Journeys of Faith

*Retracing the Faith-filled Steps of
Great Bible Characters*

Paul Chappell

Copyright © 2008 by Striving Together Publications. All Scripture quotations are taken from the King James Version.

First published in 2008 by Striving Together Publications, a ministry of Lancaster Baptist Church, Lancaster, CA 93535. Striving Together Publications is committed to providing tried, trusted, and proven books that will further equip local churches to carry out the Great Commission. Your comments and suggestions are valued.

All rights reserved. No part of this book may be reproduced, stored in a retrieval system, or transmitted in any form or by any means—electronic, mechanical, photocopy, recording, or otherwise—without written permission of the publisher, except for brief quotations in printed reviews.

Striving Together Publications
4020 E. Lancaster Blvd.
Lancaster, CA 93535
800.201.7748

Cover design by Andrew Jones
Layout by Craig Parker
Edited by Pam Oslin and Danielle Mordh
Special thanks to our proofreaders.

ISBN 978-1-59894-069-5

Printed in the United States of America

Table of Contents

How to Use This Curriculum v

Lesson One—The Journey to Ararat 1

Lesson Two—The Journey to Mount Moriah 17

Lesson Three—The Journey to the Palace 35

Lesson Four—The Journey to Egypt 53

Lesson Five—The Journey to Sinai 73

Lesson Six—The Journey to the Promised Land. 93

Lesson Seven—The Journey from Discouragement to Destiny 113

Lesson Eight—The Journey to Jericho 133

Lesson Nine—The Journey to Shiloh. 151

Lesson Ten—The Journey to the Valley of Elah 171

Lesson Eleven—The Journey to Zion. 193

Lesson Twelve—The Journey to the Cross 211

Lesson Thirteen—The Journey to the Tomb. 229

How to Use This Curriculum

Take a moment to familiarize yourself with the features of this *Striving Together* Sunday school curriculum:

Schedule

The lessons contained in this curriculum are undated, allowing you to begin and end the teaching series at any time. There are thirteen lessons that traditionally may be taught weekly any time of the year.

Student Edition Books

Companion books are available through *Striving Together Publications*. These contain:

- The outlines with blanks that students may fill in during the lessons

- Various Scripture quotations that are used throughout each lesson
- Introductory lesson overviews
- Study questions for review throughout the week
- A suggested memory verse for each lesson

These books are excellent tools for the members of a class. We suggest ordering enough books for each class member, plus additional copies for new members who enroll in the class throughout the teaching series. Giving class members a study book encourages students to be faithful to the class, provides them with a devotional tool for use throughout the week, and allows them to review what they learned previously.

Key Verses

The verses from which the lessons are taken are included at the beginning of each lesson so that you may read them through several times in prayerful preparation for your time in class. Many teachers choose to memorize their key verses. During the class hour, we suggest that you use your own Bible for Scripture reading and encourage your class members to do so as well.

Lesson Overview and Lesson Aim

The overview and aim sections are provided so that you may be aware of the overall emphasis of each lesson, especially as it relates to the other lessons in the curriculum. These brief statements provide a snapshot of where each lesson will take the students.

How to Use This Curriculum

Lesson Goals

Bible teaching has a higher goal than the delivery of information. That goal is a life-change. Students want to know what they are to do with what they are given from God's Word. As you prepare and teach each lesson, emphasize how those listening may apply its truths throughout the week.

Teaching Outline

The abbreviated outline enables you to view the entire lesson at a glance to see how the content fits together. Teaching with an organized outline increases the students' abilities to understand and remember the lesson content.

LESSON ONE

The Journey to Ararat

Key Verses

Genesis 6:1–9, 22

Lesson Overview

When God saw how wicked the people in the world had become, He was sorry that He had created them. Noah was the only one who walked with God. God warned Noah that He was going to destroy the world by a flood because of its wickedness, and He commanded him to build an ark for himself and his family. Noah obeyed without reservation. God gave him instructions for the ark, and he followed those instructions to the letter without questioning or reasoning with God. When the flood came, Noah and his family were safe in the ark. Because of Noah's obedience, God provided for and protected them.

Lesson Aim

Obedience to God is essential to a successful journey of faith, and we must be ready to obey God with a right spirit and willing heart.

Lesson Goals

At the conclusion of this lesson, students should:
- Acknowledge that a corrupt heart will lead to a corrupt life.

- Be thankful for the grace of God at work in our lives.
- Desire to be ready for any God-given task.
- Rest in the safety and security provided by God when we live in obedience to Him.
- Understand the picture of salvation found in the story of Noah.

Teaching Outline

I. The Reason for the Journey
   A. Corrupt hearts
   B. Corrupt lives

II. The Readiness for the Journey
   A. Ready because of his walk
   B. Ready because of his will

III. The Results of the Journey
   A. Preservation of the people
      1. Noah was safe in the ark.
      2. Noah was secure in the ark.
   B. Preservation of the faith
   C. Preservation of the Gospel
      1. Noah preached faith in the Word of God.
      2. The ark is a picture of our salvation.
      3. God remembered Noah.

LESSON ONE

The Journey to Ararat

Text

Genesis 6:1–9, 22

Introduction

In 1969, in Pass Christian, Mississippi, a group of people were preparing to have a "hurricane party" in the face of a storm named Camille. Were they ignorant of the dangers? Could they have been overconfident? Did they let their egos and pride influence their decision? We will never know.

What we do know is that the wind was howling outside the posh Richelieu Apartments when Police Chief Jerry Peralta pulled up sometime after dark. Facing the beach less than 250 feet from the surf, the apartments were directly in the line of the storm. A man with a drink in his hand came out to the second-floor balcony and waved. Peralta yelled up,

"You all need to clear out of here as quickly as you can. The storm's getting worse." But as others joined the man on the balcony, they just laughed at Peralta's order to leave. "This is my land," one of them yelled back. "If you want me off, you'll have to arrest me."

Peralta didn't arrest anyone, but he wasn't able to persuade them to leave either. He wrote down the names of the next of kin of the twenty or so people who gathered there to party through the storm. They laughed as he took their names. They had been warned, but they had no intention of leaving.

It was 10:15 PM when the front wall of the storm came ashore. Scientists clocked Camille's wind speed at more than 205 miles-per-hour, the strongest on record. Raindrops hit with the force of bullets, and waves off the Gulf Coast crested between twenty-two and twenty-eight feet high.

News reports later showed that the worst damage came at the little settlement of motels, go-go bars, and gambling houses known as Pass Christian, Mississippi, where some twenty people were killed at a hurricane party in the Richelieu Apartments. Nothing was left of that three-story structure but the foundation; the only survivor was a five-year-old boy found clinging to a mattress the following day.

We wonder why people are so foolish to ignore the obvious signs of coming peril. Why did they disregard the warnings that were so evident? People in our day are not much different from people in Noah's day—they are refusing to acknowledge the signs of coming judgment! Men and woman who lived during Noah's time had turned their backs on their Creator. The population was exploding, and the hearts of men were wicked. Yet, God designed a journey of grace for those who would follow Him in complete obedience.

Lesson One—The Journey to Ararat

I. The Reason for the Journey

Genesis 6:5–6

5   And GOD saw that the wickedness of man was great in the earth, and that every imagination of the thoughts of his heart was only evil continually.
6   And it repented the LORD that he had made man on the earth, and it grieved him at his heart.

Between the time of Creation and the time of Noah, extreme wickedness had developed on the earth. Man had become continually evil. God's heart was grieved to the point that He purposed to destroy the wickedness with a worldwide flood. He examined the heart of every person on the earth and found righteousness in only one—Noah. He decided to send a flood, but He would save Noah and all who would heed His warning.

Genesis 6:7–8

7   And the LORD said, I will destroy man whom I have created from the face of the earth; both man, and beast, and the creeping thing, and the fowls of the air; for it repenteth me that I have made them.
8   But Noah found grace in the eyes of the LORD.

A. Corrupt hearts (v. 5)

In the beginning, God created Adam and Eve without sin. This holiness allowed them to enjoy fellowship with God. Satan, disguised as a serpent, spoke to Eve and tempted her to disobey God's command. Eve, using her own reasoning, rationalized her disobedience. She gave the fruit of the tree to Adam, and he ate it. Because of their choice to sin, they experienced spiritual death, losing their fellowship with God.

After the fall, the population of the world began to multiply rapidly, and the inward and habitual sinfulness multiplied just as rapidly. Genesis 6:5 states that every imagination of their hearts was only evil continually. The Hebrew word for "imagination" refers to "fashioning pottery." It means to make wickedness fashionable. The people of Noah's day were truly corrupt and abominable, as the psalmist described in Psalm 14:1, "*The fool hath said in his heart, There is no God. They are corrupt, they have done abominable works, there is none that doeth good.*"

In just 1656 years (ten generations) all of humanity had become corrupt before God. God had become so grieved with the prevalent wickedness that He purposed to destroy the world with a flood.

B. Corrupt lives

A corrupt heart will always produce a corrupt life, and so was the case in Noah's day. Sin was rampant. It had become accepted, even fashionable. There seemed to be no limits or restraint. During Noah's time, sin went from being exceedingly repulsive to being tolerated and eventually accepted. However, it is important to note that our world today can be described in much the same way. Luke 17:26 says, "*And as it was in the days of Noe, so shall it be also in the days of the Son of man.*" Today, we are living in a world in which so much is built around fleshly pleasures and evil desires, and believers have become accustomed to the sin that is around them.

Noah's righteousness condemned the wicked world around him. His example of obedience to God was contrasted to the folly of the world's wickedness. By his obedience, their disobedience was exposed. Noah's holy life was an indictment of the sinfulness around him. What kind of an example are you to those around you? Are you bringing conviction to their lives by your consistent godly example? May we never grow accustomed to the blatant sinfulness of our day, and may we strive to live a holy life in the midst of a perverse and wicked culture.

II. Readiness for the Journey

The greatest decision in Noah's life was not his decision to build the ark; it was his decision to walk with God. Before God can use you greatly, He must prepare you greatly. Noah was a man who was prepared and ready for an assignment from God. He developed a true relationship with God that prepared him for the journey of faith on which he would embark.

A. *Ready because of his walk*

GENESIS 6:8–9

8   But Noah found grace in the eyes of the LORD.
9   These are the generations of Noah: Noah was a just man and perfect in his generations, and Noah walked with God.

While the world was only wicked continually, Noah was walking with God consistently. Contrary to the culture of his day, Noah chose to cultivate a personal relationship with God, and by daily walking with Him, Noah's life was transformed into one of exceptional character that prepared him for his journey to Ararat.

Are you walking daily with your Saviour? Are you purposefully developing a meaningful relationship with Him? John 15:3–4 says, "*Now ye are clean through the word which I have spoken unto you.* **Abide** *in me, and I in you. As* *the branch cannot bear fruit of itself, except it abide in the vine; no more can ye, except ye abide in me."*

Worshiping God was not just something Noah did on Sundays. It was a part of his daily life. God did not choose Noah to build the ark because of the things that he did for Him. He chose to use Noah because of who he was before Him. A Christian's life is not measured by how much he does but by who he is. May we determine to be something before God before attempting to do things for Him. May we prepare for the Master's use through cultivating a walk with God.

B. Ready because of his will
GENESIS 6:22
22 *Thus did Noah; according to all that God commanded him, so did he.*

God honored Noah because of his obedient spirit. He was a man who practiced daily obedience to God. When God told Noah to build the ark, there was no question that he would obey. He had determined to respond to God in all things. Obedience to God was not a decision that had to be made every time a new situation arose. He had decided early in life to obey God.

Illustration
Roger Staubach who led the Dallas Cowboys to the World Championship in '71 admitted that his position as a quarterback who didn't call his own signals was a source of struggle for him. Coach Landry sent in every play. He told Roger when to pass, when to run and only in emergency situations could he change the play. Even

though Roger considered Coach Landry to have a "genius mind" when it came to football strategy, pride said that he should be able to run his own team.

Roger later said, "I faced up to the issue of obedience. Once I learned to obey, there was harmony, fulfillment, and victory."

If we want harmony, fulfillment, and victory in our lives, we must learn to obey as well! God wants us to obey His Word. Psalm 119:105 says, "*Thy word is a lamp unto my feet, and a light unto my path.*" God will guide and direct us as we allow His Word to illuminate our steps along the journey. The Word of God is reliable and provides answers for those who reproach us. Psalm 119:42 says, "*So shall I have wherewith to answer him that reproacheth me: for I trust in thy word.*" Surely Noah suffered reproach for obeying God! Yet, he faithfully continued to obey God out of a heart of fear—a heart of reverential trust.

When the fear of God is gone, the decisions of daily life are threatened. When you are walking in obedience to God, the choices will already be made before the difficult decisions come. You will choose to follow Him. When God has a task for you, you will not analyze, question, or doubt. The decision was already made when you purposed to obey.

Noah's will was bent toward obeying God. How is your will? Do you have a determination to obey God no matter the cost?

III. The Results of the Journey

God's holiness demands judgment. However, He always provides a way of escape. Noah told others of the coming flood and pleaded for men to repent, but they would not. The people of Noah's day chose to ignore the witness of God. The flood destroyed all human life that was not safe in the ark. Yet, God did not end the human race forever. There was one righteous man! Noah found grace in the eyes of the Lord.

Noah's decision to build and enter the ark was instrumental in the preservation of the human race. Had he refused to obey God, the results of this journey would be drastically different.

A. *Preservation of the people*

Genesis 6:14
14 Make thee an ark of gopher wood; rooms shalt thou make in the ark, and shalt pitch it within and without with pitch.

Genesis 7:1
1 And the Lord said unto Noah, Come thou and all thy house into the ark; for thee have I seen righteous before me in this generation.

God's grace was clearly displayed to all who lived during Noah's time. It was seen in His warning of a coming flood, His invitation to join Noah on the ark, and His provision for a way of escape. However, only Noah and his family decided to obey God, and because of this, they were safe in the ark. When we follow God in complete trust and obedience, we can rest in the safety He provides. Proverbs 3:5–6 say, *"Trust in the Lord with all thine heart; and lean not unto thine own understanding. In all thy ways acknowledge him, and he shall direct thy paths."*

Lesson One—The Journey to Ararat

Noah was also secure in the ark. Genesis 7:16 states, *"And they that went in, went in male and female of all flesh, as God had commanded him: and the LORD shut him in."* What a comfort it must have been to Noah to know that God had shut the door to the ark! He and his family must have keenly experienced the safety and security of God in a very special way. In a day when situations and institutions (such as the economy and government) give cause for great insecurity, we can trust in the security of our God! Just as He did with Noah, He will preserve us and keep us safe and secure as we follow His will.

B. Preservation of the faith
GENESIS 6:9
9 These are the generations of Noah: Noah was a just man and perfect in his generations, and Noah walked with God.

The Bible calls Noah a preacher of righteousness. Although only his family chose to heed the warning, Noah still proclaimed the truth of the coming judgment. Second Peter 2:5 says, *"And spared not the old world, but saved Noah the eighth person, a preacher of righteousness, bringing in the flood upon the world of the ungodly."* God offered the journey of grace to those who would follow Him out of a heart of belief.

The wicked lineage mentioned in our passage had spread throughout the world, but Noah was perfect in his generations. Therefore, God designed a way for Noah and the people of his day to escape the coming judgment. Ezekiel 14:14 says, *"Though these three men, Noah, Daniel, and Job, were in it, they should deliver but their own souls by their righteousness, saith the Lord*

GOD." God will preserve those who walk in His way. By sparing Noah and his family, God preserved the faith for future generations.

C. Preservation of the Gospel

Not only did God preserve the people and the faith of Noah, He also preserved the Gospel. This biblical account of Noah and the ark provides a clear picture and example of salvation!

Noah preached faith in the Word of God. Hebrews 11:7 says, *"By faith Noah, being warned of God of things not seen as yet, moved with fear, prepared an ark to the saving of his house; by the which he condemned the world, and became heir of the righteousness which is by faith."* Noah condemned the worldliness of his day, and in choosing to believe God, he became an heir of righteousness through his faith.

The ark is a picture of our salvation! First Peter 3:20 says, *"Which sometime were disobedient, when once the longsuffering of God waited in the days of Noah, while the ark was a preparing, wherein few, that is, eight souls were saved by water."* We see the love of God in His longsuffering. God was patient with those who chose not to believe, but once the ark was complete, a choice had to be made in order to be saved. We see the way of God through the single door in the ark. There was only one door on the ark for those who chose to enter. In the same way, there is only one way to Heaven! John 10:9 says, *"I am the door: by me if any man enter in, he shall be saved, and shall go in and out, and find pasture."* We also see the faithfulness of God in keeping His promise to save us. God is not slack concerning His promise, and we can trust Him to take us to Heaven!

We also see that God remembered Noah. Genesis 8:1 declares: *"And God remembered Noah, and every living thing, and all the cattle that was with him in the ark: and God made a wind to pass over the earth, and the waters asswaged."* God brought Noah's journey of faith to a safe and wonderful end on the mountain top of Ararat. We can thank the Lord that when our earthly journey is through, He will remember us and bring us safely home to Heaven.

Conclusion

MATTHEW 24:37–39
37 *But as the days of Noe were, so shall also the coming of the Son of man be.*
38 *For as in the days that were before the flood they were eating and drinking, marrying and giving in marriage, until the day that Noe entered into the ark,*
39 *And knew not until the flood came, and took them all away; so shall also the coming of the Son of man be.*

The times in which we live are very much the same as the times in which Noah was living for the Lord. May we learn from Noah's journey to Ararat.

Noah claimed the grace of God to obey in daunting circumstances. Though it may have seemed otherwise, God did not ask Noah to do the impossible! In himself, Noah did not have the strength and knowledge to do the work God called him to do. Nevertheless, God supplied the grace Noah needed to accomplish the task. When God gives you an undertaking, He will supply the grace needed to successfully accomplish the work. Second Corinthians 9:8 says, *"And God is able to make all grace abound toward you; that ye, always having all sufficiency in all things, may abound to every good work."* During our journeys of faith, God wants us to acknowledge our weaknesses and depend on Him as we strive to follow Him in obedience. Second Corinthians 12:9 provides us with this promise: *"And he said unto me, My grace is sufficient for thee: for my strength is made perfect in weakness...."*

Noah also obeyed God completely. He built the ark faithfully day after day. He did not worry about the things he did not understand. He continued faithfully executing the job God had given him to do. He did not refuse to begin until all of the questions were answered. He did not have to see all the details worked out. He followed every instruction God had given him and left the rest to God.

During days of wickedness on the earth, Noah found favor and kindness in the eyes of the Lord. Genesis 6:8 says, *"But Noah found grace in the eyes of the Lord."* How can we live our lives in this wicked generation so we can find grace in the eyes of the Lord? Follow Noah's example. Choose to embark on the journey of faith. Follow God in complete obedience and choose to claim His promises when you become weary. Then, when your journey is over and you arrive safely at Ararat, may you praise Him for His grace and guidance along the way!

2 Peter 3:9

9   *The Lord is not slack concerning his promise, as some men count slackness; but is longsuffering to us-ward, not willing that any should perish, but that all should come to repentance.*

Lesson One—The Journey to Ararat

Study Questions

1. Why did God regret that He had created the world? What did He decide to do as a result?
   God regretted that He created the world because the people were living in continual wickedness. They had corrupt hearts and lives.

   God judged the world by sending a flood.

2. In our text, what does the Hebrew word for "imagination" refer to? Explain what it means in the context of the passage we are studying.
   It refers to fashioning pottery and means that they were making wickedness fashionable.

3. What does a corrupt heart always lead to?
   A corrupt heart will always lead to a corrupt life.

4. How can people today escape God's judgment?
   People of today can escape judgment by believing in Jesus and receiving Him as Saviour.

5. How was Noah ready for his journey?
   Noah prepared for his journey of obedience by cultivating a right will and right walk before the Lord.

6. How did God preserve Noah as a result of his obedience?
   The Lord preserved Noah by providing the safety and security of the ark.

7. List the pictures of salvation that we find in the story of Noah.
   We see the love of God in His longsuffering.

   We see the way to God through the single door in the ark.

   We see the faithfulness of God in keeping His promise to save us.

8. Take a moment to identify areas in your life in which God is calling you to obedience. Are you willing and ready to obey? List the steps you must take to follow God in complete obedience to Him.
   Answers will vary.

Memory Verse

2 Peter 3:9

9 The Lord is not slack concerning his promise, as some men count slackness; but is longsuffering to us-ward, not willing that any should perish, but that all should come to repentance.

LESSON TWO

The Journey to Mount Moriah

Key Verses

Genesis 22:1–19

Lesson Overview

God tested Abraham many times during his lifetime, but the greatest test came when God told Abraham to sacrifice his son Isaac. Abraham did not question or resist. He simply responded in obedience. When Abraham and his son reached Mount Moriah, he built an altar and laid Isaac upon it. As Abraham raised the knife, God knew that there was no end to Abraham's love and obedience. As a result, He provided a ram to sacrifice instead.

Lesson Aim

When God calls us to testing and sacrifice, our response should be one of immediate and faithful obedience, trusting Him to bring about His desired result in our lives.

Lesson Goals

At the conclusion of this lesson, students should:
- Realize that trials and testing are a part of the Christian life.
- Strive to respond to God's commands with obedience.
- Prepare to be ready to sacrifice for the Lord.

- Trust God to meet their needs as they respond to Him in obedience.

Teaching Outline

I. The Request from the Lord
   A. A call to testing
   B. A call to sacrifice
      1. The promised seed
      2. The promised son

II. The Response of Obedience
   A. Immediate obedience
   B. Faithful obedience

III. The Result of Faith
   A. Abraham prepares to sacrifice.
   B. God provides a replacement.

LESSON TWO

The Journey to Mount Moriah

Text

Genesis 22:1–19

Introduction

Every day, we express faith in many different ways—whether by taking a prescription from the doctor, flying in an airplane, or ordering at a fast food restaurant! We express faith in the people who render their services to us on a daily basis. Most of the time, we give it no thought at all.

As Christians, it is easy for us to follow God's commands when things are going our way. Yet, as soon as an instruction comes that is contrary to our nature, or that seems utterly impossible, our faith tends to waver drastically.

The Bible says that Abraham was a great man of faith:

Hebrews 11:8–10

8 By faith Abraham, when he was called to go out into a place which he should after receive for an inheritance, obeyed; and he went out, not knowing whither he went.

9 By faith he sojourned in the land of promise, as in a strange country, dwelling in tabernacles with Isaac and Jacob, the heirs with him of the same promise:

10 For he looked for a city which hath foundations, whose builder and maker is God.

> **TEACHING TIP**
>
> *The word "called" in verse 8 comes from the Greek word* kalewkaleo *which means "to call" or "to invite." God invited Abraham on a journey of faith.*

Abraham was called by God to leave the land of his father, the Ur of the Chaldees (modern day Iraq). Abraham responded to God out of a heart of belief in this single instance of faith. He obeyed without delay or question. God was testing Abraham's confidence in Him, and He was taking Abraham on a journey to strengthen His faith.

> **TEACHING TIP**
>
> *The word "obeyed" comes from the Greek word* upakouw, hupakouo *and means "to listen, to hearken to a command, to submit to."*

Trusting God to provide a son was another step in Abraham's personal journey of faith. To all human reasoning, the birth of Isaac appeared impossible, but the strength of Abraham's faith was demonstrated by simple confidence in

Lesson Two—The Journey to Mount Moriah

God. Our journey of faith will often lead us, as well, to the doorstep of the impossible. Nevertheless, our confidence should not be shaken. God's ability to answer prayer does not depend on our limited human reasoning.

Abraham had waited many years for God to fulfill the promise of a son, and it seemed as though all possibility of bearing a child was gone. Abraham was ninety-nine years old, and there was still no son of promise. Yet, God came to Abraham and reminded him of the promises He had given:

GENESIS 17:16–17
16 And I will bless her, and give thee a son also of her: yea, I will bless her, and she shall be a mother of nations; kings of people shall be of her.
17 Then Abraham fell upon his face, and laughed, and said in his heart, Shall a child be born unto him that is an hundred years old? and shall Sarah, that is ninety years old, bear?

Finally, Isaac, God's promised child, had come! God was faithful to remember Abraham and Sarah. Undoubtedly this fulfilled promise brought great joy to their lives. In this lesson, however, we will learn from the supreme test of Abraham's faith. God required from Abraham absolute trust and a complete willingness to sacrifice his hopes and dreams of a great nation. His journey to Mount Moriah would be the ultimate test of his faith.

I. The Request from the Lord

GENESIS 22:1–2
1 And it came to pass after these things, that God did tempt Abraham, and said unto him, Abraham: and he said, Behold, here I am.

2 And he said, Take now thy son, thine only son Isaac, whom thou lovest, and get thee into the land of Moriah; and offer him there for a burnt offering upon one of the mountains which I will tell thee of.

Though the request to sacrifice Isaac was perhaps the greatest test of Abraham's faith, it was not the first. Genesis records three major trials he faced, his response to the trials, and God's subsequent blessing and continued faithfulness.

The record of Abraham's testing in the Bible allows us to follow one man's journey of faith. His response to God illustrates a journey filled with right decisions and God's provision. Through the trial of his faith, Abraham had proven himself true to God.

A. *A call to testing (v. 1)*

God told Abraham to go to Moriah, which was about a three-day journey.

When God called Abraham to offer his son Isaac on the altar, it was an evaluation of his soul's commitment to God. How he responded to this test would reveal his true heart condition.

Lesson Two—The Journey to Mount Moriah

The Bible says God tempted Abraham (Genesis 22:1). In our day, the word *tempted* often implies an enticement to do evil. However, in Genesis 22, the meaning is "to try" or "to prove." It is important to note that God does not tempt us to sin. James says, *"Let no man say when he is tempted, I am tempted of God: for God cannot be tempted with evil, neither tempteth he any man: But every man is tempted, when he is drawn away of his own lust, and enticed. Then when lust hath conceived, it bringeth forth sin: and sin, when it is finished, bringeth forth death"* (James 1:13–15).

God works to bring us closer to Him. You see, true faith goes into operation when there are no answers to be found, and God uses trying circumstances to stretch our faith and draw us closer to Him.

1 Peter 1:7
7   That the trial of your faith, being much more precious than of gold that perisheth, though it be tried with fire, might be found unto praise and honour and glory at the appearing of Jesus Christ:

B. A call to sacrifice (v. 2)

In this verse, we see that Abraham was asked to sacrifice that which was dear to him. Isaac was the promised seed mentioned in Genesis 15:5–6.

Genesis 15:5–6
5   And he brought him forth abroad, and said, Look now toward heaven, and tell the stars, if thou be able to number them: and he said unto him, So shall thy seed be.
6   And he believed in the Lord; and he counted it to him for righteousness.

When Isaac finally arrived, he was a daily joy and reminder of God's faithfulness and blessing. Abraham and Sarah were not surrounded with many children. Isaac was their only child, and the one whom God had promised would have numerous descendants. Abraham had only one son through which this divine promise could be fulfilled.

Isaac was not only the promised seed, he was also the promised son. God had miraculously provided a son for Abraham. (Notice God asks for his "only son" in verse two. Ishmael was not the son God had promised to Abraham and had already been sent away.) Abraham and Sarah thought they were too old to have a son, but God kept His promise.

Illustration

Someone once said, "You know you're getting older when in the morning you hear snap, crackle, pop, and it isn't your breakfast cereal!" I'm sure Sarah had a few aches and pains herself as she grew older, and she was definitely past the age of giving birth! Yet, God remained faithful to fulfill His promise.

HEBREWS 11:11–12

11 *Through faith also Sarah herself received strength to conceive seed, and was delivered of a child when she was past age, because she judged him faithful who had promised.*

12 *Therefore sprang there even of one, and him as good as dead, so many as the stars of the sky in multitude, and as the sand which is by the sea shore innumerable.*

II. The Response of Obedience

GENESIS 22:3–8

3 And Abraham rose up early in the morning, and saddled his ass, and took two of his young men with him, and Isaac his son, and clave the wood for the burnt offering, and rose up, and went unto the place of which God had told him.
4 Then on the third day Abraham lifted up his eyes, and saw the place afar off.
5 And Abraham said unto his young men, Abide ye here with the ass; and I and the lad will go yonder and worship, and come again to you.
6 And Abraham took the wood of the burnt offering, and laid it upon Isaac his son; and he took the fire in his hand, and a knife; and they went both of them together.
7 And Isaac spake unto Abraham his father, and said, My father: and he said, Here am I, my son. And he said, Behold the fire and the wood: but where is the lamb for a burnt offering?
8 And Abraham said, My son, God will provide himself a lamb for a burnt offering: so they went both of them together.

A. *Immediate obedience (vv. 3–7)*

When God called Abraham, there was no hesitation. Abraham did not ask for a reason. He acted in complete faith and gathered everything needed to obey God entirely. Abraham prepared to offer Isaac on the altar.

George Mueller said, "Faith does not operate in the realm of the possible. There is no glory for God in that which is humanly possible. Faith begins where man's power ends."

ROMANS 1:17

17 For therein is the righteousness of God revealed from faith to faith: as it is written, The just shall live by faith.

The calmness in which Abraham expressed his obedience was due to his total trust in God. In verse 5, he told his servants that he would come again unto them. God had promised that through Isaac's seed, Abraham's people would proceed, and Abraham chose to believe in faith. D.L. Moody once said, "I prayed for faith and it did not come, but when I read the Word of God then faith came." Abraham trusted the words of God and acted in obedience to His Word.

Hebrews 11:17–19
17 By faith Abraham, when he was tried, offered up Isaac: and he that had received the promises offered up his only begotten son,
18 Of whom it was said, That in Isaac shall thy seed be called:
19 Accounting that God was able to raise him up, even from the dead; from whence also he received him in a figure.

We learn from our text that Isaac was obedient, as well. He carried the wood along his journey to Mount Moriah, picturing Christ and the cross He carried to Golgotha.

John 19:17
17 And he bearing his cross went forth into a place called the place of a skull, which is called in the Hebrew Golgotha:

It is also interesting to note that Abraham left his servants and supplies at the base of the hill when he went to worship. As Christians today, there are things we must leave behind when we come to worship Christ. We must cast off the weights that would hinder us from focusing our attention and directing our worship toward Him.

B. Faithful obedience (v. 8)

Abraham reminded his son that God would provide a sacrifice for the offering. What a true example of faithful obedience! Abraham had obeyed God before, and he was confident that he could obey God in this situation as well.

Illustration

Faith in God makes great optimists. Several years ago in Burma, Adoniram Judson was lying in a filthy jail cell with thirty-two pounds of chains on his ankles and his feet bound to a bamboo pole. With a sneer on his face, a fellow prisoner said, "Dr. Judson, what about the prospect of the conversion of the heathen?" His instant reply was, "The prospects are just as bright as the promises of God."

HEBREWS 11:1–3
1 Now faith is the substance of things hoped for, the evidence of things not seen.
2 For by it the elders obtained a good report.
3 Through faith we understand that the worlds were framed by the word of God, so that things which are seen were not made of things which do appear.

HEBREWS 11:6
6 But without faith it is impossible to please him: for he that cometh to God must believe that he is, and that he is a rewarder of them that diligently seek him.

III. The Result of Faith

Does God try us simply to see how much pressure we can handle? Does He test us to determine how strong our faith is? God knows the strength of our faith. He tests us to build our faith, to be an example to other believers, and to increase our spiritual capacity to enjoy a meaningful relationship with Him.

2 CORINTHIANS 1:3–4
3   Blessed be God, even the Father of our Lord Jesus Christ, the Father of mercies, and the God of all comfort;
4   Who comforteth us in all our tribulation, that we may be able to comfort them which are in any trouble, by the comfort wherewith we ourselves are comforted of God.

A. Abraham prepares to sacrifice.
GENESIS 22:9–10
9   And they came to the place which God had told him of; and Abraham built an altar there, and laid the wood in order, and bound Isaac his son, and laid him on the altar upon the wood.
10   And Abraham stretched forth his hand, and took the knife to slay his son.

Here, Abraham finds himself at the moral elevation of his trial; however, he proved himself willing to give his most precious possession to God. Even so, God was willing to give His only begotten Son for us. Isaac, as a picture of Christ, willingly lay down on the altar (verse 9). Christ willingly laid down His life as a sacrifice for our sins.

PHILIPPIANS 2:7–8
7   But made himself of no reputation, and took upon him the form of a servant, and was made in the likeness of men:

8 And being found in fashion as a man, he humbled himself, and became obedient unto death, even the death of the cross.

God was well pleased with Abraham's faith and promised to bless him.

GENESIS 22:15–18
15 And the angel of the LORD called unto Abraham out of heaven the second time,
16 And said, By myself have I sworn, saith the LORD, for because thou hast done this thing, and hast not withheld thy son, thine only son:
17 That in blessing I will bless thee, and in multiplying I will multiply thy seed as the stars of the heaven, and as the sand which is upon the sea shore; and thy seed shall possess the gate of his enemies;
18 And in thy seed shall all the nations of the earth be blessed; because thou hast obeyed my voice.

Is a willingness to sacrifice an evident result of the faith in your life? Like Abraham, are we willing to serve and honor the Lord with the things in life which we hold dear? Are we reluctant to sacrifice our time or talents or treasures when called upon by God to do so? May we all prepare to sacrifice for our Saviour.

B. *God provides a replacement.*

GENESIS 22:11–14
11 And the angel of the LORD called unto him out of heaven, and said, Abraham, Abraham: and he said, Here am I.
12 And he said, Lay not thine hand upon the lad, neither do thou any thing unto him: for now I know that thou fearest

God, seeing thou hast not withheld thy son, thine only son from me.

13 And Abraham lifted up his eyes, and looked, and behold behind him a ram caught in a thicket by his horns: and Abraham went and took the ram, and offered him up for a burnt offering in the stead of his son.

14 And Abraham called the name of that place Jehovah-jireh: as it is said to this day, In the mount of the LORD it shall be seen.

It is important to remember: "God is much more likely to reward our obedience with an explanation than He is to give an explanation to encourage our obedience." So often in life, we demand explanations from God; however, He is more likely to bless our trust and obedience than He is our half-hearted and doubtful obedience. In our story, we learn that God rewarded Abraham's faith and obedience with a replacement—a ram caught in the thicket.

Isaac was spared, and a ram caught in the thicket was provided in his place for the offering. By providing a replacement, God preserved Isaac and the entire nation of Israel.

Jehovah-jireh means "the Lord hath provided." God provided for Abraham, and He has provided for us as well! May we never forget that God has provided a Lamb for us, and His Lamb offers atonement for our sins. Jesus is our Lamb of sacrifice. John 1:36 says, *"And looking upon Jesus as he walked, he saith, Behold the Lamb of God!"* We can thank the Lord that Jesus took our place on the Cross. Because He provided a replacement, we can be confident of a future home in Heaven.

Lesson Two—The Journey to Mount Moriah

Illustration

Lauren McCain was one of the students killed at Virginia Tech on April 16, 2007. The freshman from Shawnee, Oklahoma, left a powerful statement about her faith on her personal web site. The 20-year-old had written, "The purpose and love of my life is Jesus Christ. I don't have to argue religion, philosophy, or historical evidence because I KNOW Him."

1 Peter 1:18–19

18 Forasmuch as ye know that ye were not redeemed with corruptible things, as silver and gold, from your vain conversation received by tradition from your fathers;
19 But with the precious blood of Christ, as of a lamb without blemish and without spot:

Conclusion

Luther Bridgers, a pastor in the early 1900s, his wife, and three boys were visiting family in Kentucky. Travel over the rough Kentucky roads brought them to the home of Mrs. Bridger's parents where the happy reunion ended rather late. Worn out from the trip and excitement, all fell asleep quickly that night. A restless neighbor glanced out the window and saw the Bridgers' home engulfed in flames. Running to wake the family, the neighbor was only able to wake the grandparents and Pastor Bridgers. Realizing his wife and three boys were still in the home, Pastor Bridgers attempted to rescue them, only to be restrained as the house crumbled in flames. When the fire was over, Luther Bridgers' wife and three boys were dead. What a tragedy! During the days of darkness and sorrow, Pastor Bridgers remembered the promise of the Lord found in Job 35:10, *"But none saith, Where is God my maker, who giveth songs in the night."* It was during this time of heartache that Luther Bridgers wrote "He Keeps Me Singing." We can see how this pastor came through the testing not with bitterness and questions but with greater strength and joy.

Just as Luther Bridgers responded correctly to God's test in his life, Abraham also walked his journey of faith in a way that was pleasing to the Lord. Abraham's faith to follow God enabled him to see His mighty hand at work.

God is still looking for people who will trust Him completely. We are all on a journey of faith, and we will all experience trials and testings. Will your journey lead you to higher ground because of your trust in Christ and obedience to Him?

Lesson Two—The Journey to Mount Moriah

Study Questions

1. According to Genesis 17:16–17, what did God promise to Abraham and Sarah?
   God promised to give Sarah a son, and also promised that she would be the mother of nations.

2. On a scale of 1–10, rate your obedience to the Lord. Identify specific steps you can take to increase your level of obedience.
   Answers will vary.

3. According to Hebrews 11:6, what one element is required in order to please God?
   Without faith, it is impossible to please God.

4. Has God required you to sacrifice something of significance in your life? How did you respond?
   Answers will vary.

5. What does "Jehovah-Jireh" mean?
   The Lord hath provided.

6. How did God provide for Abraham? How has God provided salvation for us?
   God provided a ram to take Isaac's place on the altar. God has provided salvation for us by giving His son, Jesus, to take our place on the Cross.

7. When Abraham began his journey to worship the Lord on Mount Moriah, he left his supplies and servants at the base of the mountain. Identify any hindrances that need to be left behind in your life and briefly describe

what actions you will take to remove these hindrances to your worship.
Answers will vary.

8. Are you trusting God to provide for your needs, as did Abraham? Take a moment and write a prayer to the Lord, expressing your confidence and trust in Him and thanking Him for being a trustworthy God.
Answers will vary.

Memory Verse

1 Corinthians 10:13

13 There hath no temptation taken you but such as is common to man: but God is faithful, who will not suffer you to be tempted above that ye are able; but will with the temptation also make a way to escape, that ye may be able to bear it.

LESSON THREE

The Journey to the Palace

Key Verses
Exodus 1:1–22, Exodus 2:1–10

Lesson Overview
Pharaoh issued a decree that all baby boys born to the Hebrews in captivity were to be killed at birth. Amram and Jochebed were blessed with a baby boy, Moses. With love and courage, Moses' mother Jochebed placed Moses in a small waterproof basket and hid him in the Nile River. As he was hidden, the princess of Egypt came to the river. She heard the baby cry, sent her maids to find him, and took pity on the child. Moses' sister Miriam perceived what was happening and offered to find a nurse for the child. When the princess agreed, Miriam quickly ran to get Jochebed. The princess hired Jochebed, Moses' own mother, to raise this Hebrew baby for her. God protected Moses and provided his own mother to raise and train him to follow God's purposes for his life.

Lesson Aim
As Christians, we must trust the provision of the Lord and seek to fulfill the purposes given to us by God. As parents, we must protect our homes from the threat of evil and provide a Christ-honoring, loving environment for our children as

we seek to raise them to discover God's unique purposes for their own lives.

Lesson Goals

At the conclusion of this lesson, students should:
- Develop a heart to protect their families from Satan's attacks.
- Determine to trust God's provision in spite of trying circumstances.
- Follow God's principles for raising children.
- Choose to identify with God and God's people.
- Trust God to reward obedience.

Teaching Outline

I. The Protection of Jochabed
    A. From the threat of evil
    B. From the attack of Satan
        1. Set boundaries.
        2. Give warning.
        3. Set an example.
        4. Be wise to that which is good.
        5. Teach the Word of God.
        6. Practice forgiveness.

II. The Provision of the Lord
    A. He provided a place for Moses.
    B. He provides principles for us.
        1. Nurture
        2. Admonition

III. The Purpose of Moses
    A. To identify with God's people
    B. To separate from sin
    C. To wait on God's reward

LESSON THREE

The Journey to the Palace

Text
Exodus 1:1–22, Exodus 2:1–10

Introduction
In our world today, the media belittles biblical family values. Motherhood does not get much encouragement from our society. The feminist movement deplores the concept of a mom staying at home, and the crowd who defends abortion rights sends a message about motherhood that is undesirable. In reality, motherhood is the most influential role on planet earth!

Illustration
A school teacher gave her class of second-graders a lesson on magnets and how they have the ability to pick objects up off

the ground. The next day the teacher gave her kids a pop quiz. She said, "My name has six letters and I pick up things. What am I?" When the test papers were turned in, the teacher was surprised to find that almost half of her students answered the question not with the word *magnet* but with the word *mother*. The children had concluded that *mothers* pick up things—not *magnets*.

Illustration

Newsweek stated that the average mom at home works ninety-two hours a week. Another study found that if a typical mother were paid for all the duties she did in the home, she would earn an average of $138,095 a year in the business world. This figure comes from the tasks accomplished by a mother in an average day. You see, in an average day a mother can be a taxi cab driver, a counselor, an engineer, a carpenter, an accountant, a judge, a motivational speaker, a teacher, a chef, a supervisor, a personal assistant, an event coordinator, an administrator, and a preacher. You combine all those jobs together, and you couldn't pay a mother enough. Paying $138,095 a year sounds cheap. The work that most mothers do is priceless! (Newsweek.com, May 14, 2007)

The Bible says that a virtuous woman, a godly mother, is priceless!

PROVERBS 31:10

10 Who can find a virtuous woman? for her price is far above rubies.

PROVERBS 31:28

28 Her children arise up, and call her blessed; her husband also, and he praiseth her.

Lesson Three—The Journey to the Palace

Moses was born into a wicked world during the time of the Egyptian bondage. During this period in history, the Jews suffered four hundred years of difficulties. One of the greatest trials and most reprehensible acts committed by the Pharoah was his command to the Jewish midwives to kill the male babies as they were born. Moses' mother Jochabed acted wisely in the face of great danger. There is much to be learned from her journey of faith.

I. The Protection of Jochabed

Exodus 2:1–5

1 And there went a man of the house of Levi, and took to wife a daughter of Levi.
2 And the woman conceived, and bare a son: and when she saw him that he was a goodly child, she hid him three months.
3 And when she could not longer hide him, she took for him an ark of bulrushes, and daubed it with slime and with pitch, and put the child therein; and she laid it in the flags by the river's brink.
4 And his sister stood afar off, to wit what would be done to him.
5 And the daughter of Pharaoh came down to wash herself at the river; and her maidens walked along by the river's side; and when she saw the ark among the flags, she sent her maid to fetch it.

Jochebed had a child named Moses whom she wanted to protect from Pharaoh's evil command to kill all baby boys. God's plan, however, went beyond merely protecting the baby from death. It involved giving Moses the foundation to be a man greatly used by God. From our text, we gain a glimpse of Moses' childhood as he begins his journey for the faith.

PROVERBS 1:8

8 *My son, hear the instruction of thy father, and forsake not the law of thy mother:*

A. *From the threat of evil*

Jochebed hid Moses from the evil influence that threatened him.

HEBREWS 11:23

23 *By faith Moses, when he was born, was hid three months of his parents, because they saw he was a proper child; and they were not afraid of the king's commandment.*

Wickedness in Moses' day threatened to eliminate God's chosen people. While Pharoah was planning the extermination of the Jewish people, God was preparing their emancipation in the protection of baby Moses. God not only saved Moses from death, but He had a special mission for him to accomplish—a purpose given to him at birth. He was to be the leader of Israel, and God would guide him every step of the way on his journey for the faith.

The faith of Jochebed gave her the courage to protect Moses from the threat of evil. She chose to put her life in danger in order to preserve and shelter Moses from the threat of wickedness. Hidden in a small basket on the Nile River, Moses was protected from Pharaoh's order. God's hand was evident as the princess felt pity for the child. She further insured Moses' protection from Pharaoh's wicked command.

Just as Satan attempted to destroy the Jewish race in Jochebed's day, he is trying to eliminate future generations of Christians today. Yet, even when evil is rampant, God is willing and able to lead and protect his children on their journey.

B. From the attack of Satan

Jochebed not only protected Moses from the threat of evil, she also protected him from a direct attack from Satan. Satan's purpose was to destroy the entire nation of Israel and he was accomplishing it by attacking the family. (If all the male children were killed that would eliminate the future generations.) Satan is trying to destroy the Christian family in our world today by turning the hearts of children against their parents and infiltrating their lives with wickedness.

In this evil day, God is calling parents to be like Jochebed—willing to protect their families from the evil that is so prevalent in our society. There are several key ways in which we can protect our children:

1. Set boundaries.
PROVERBS 4:1–2

1   Hear, ye children, the instruction of a father, and attend to know understanding.
2   For I give you good doctrine, forsake ye not my law.

Illustration

One student gave a humorous definition of a grandmother: "Someone who comes to visit and keeps your mother from spanking you!"

While this definition may be true in many cases, God has still placed authority into His institutions. The family is God's institution, and as parents, we are required to establish boundaries for our children.

Standards and guidelines are not designed to rob joy; they are designed to protect.

2. Give warning
PROVERBS 1:7
7   The fear of the LORD is the beginning of knowledge: but fools despise wisdom and instruction.

Illustration

Keri was four years old and an incessant talker. This made it difficult for her parents and even her grandparents when it was time to put her to bed at night. One evening, Keri's grandfather was putting her to bed, but she just wasn't ready to stop talking. She had said her prayers, been tucked in, and had been told "good-night," but she wasn't ready to be quiet! Her grandfather reminded her again that it was time to stop talking and go to sleep, to which little Keri replied, "But Papa, my mouth is not empty yet!"

The average parent will readily admit that when it comes to giving warning, they do it often! However, it is important to remember the following quote: "Strictness does not ruin children. Harshness ruins children."

As parents, we must ask God for wisdom to be strict, but not harsh in our warnings as we strive to protect our children.

3. Set an example
2 TIMOTHY 1:5
5   When I call to remembrance the unfeigned faith that is in thee, which dwelt first in thy grandmother Lois, and thy mother Eunice; and I am persuaded that in thee also.

Lesson Three—The Journey to the Palace

We've all heard the saying (and have probably repeated the saying), "Do as I say. Don't do as I do!" Children, however, may not always do as you say, but they almost always do as you do!

In making an effort to protect our children from Satan's attacks, it is imperative that we maintain a consistent and godly example before them in all areas of life.

4. Be wise to that which is good.
ROMANS 16:19
19 For your obedience is come abroad unto all men. I am glad therefore on your behalf: but yet I would have you wise unto that which is good, and simple concerning evil.

Illustration

A grandmother was trying to teach her grandsons not to be so mean to girls. Two of her grandsons were playing marbles when a pretty little girl walked by. "I'll tell you," said Jake to JD, "when I stop hating girls, that's the one I'm going to stop hating first."

Even at a young age, we need to teach our children to be wise concerning that which is good. The world is doing a very good job at advertising that which is evil, and sadly many young people are very knowledgeable about the wickedness of our day. May we do our part as parents to uplift and teach that which is good.

5. Teach the Word of God.
DEUTERONOMY 6:6–7
6 And these words, which I command thee this day, shall be in thine heart:

7 And thou shalt teach them diligently unto thy children, and shalt talk of them when thou sittest in thine house, and when thou walkest by the way, and when thou liest down, and when thou risest up.

Teaching God's Word to our children is essential. The Bible is our sword and main source of protection against the evils of this world.

In Deuteronomy, we find the command to diligently teach our children from the Scriptures. If your teaching cannot be described as diligent and purposeful, perhaps an adjustment should be made for the sake of your children's protection.

6. Practice forgiveness.
EPHESIANS 4:32

32 And be ye kind one to another, tenderhearted, forgiving one another, even as God for Christ's sake hath forgiven you.

May our children always rest in the security of our forgiveness. How we thank the Lord for the forgiveness He has shown to us! Yet, we must also express that same forgiveness to our children. May they rest in the comfort and protection that our forgiveness can provide.

II. The Provision of the Lord

EXODUS 2:5–9

5 And the daughter of Pharaoh came down to wash herself at the river; and her maidens walked along by the river's side; and when she saw the ark among the flags, she sent her maid to fetch it.

Lesson Three—The Journey to the Palace

6 And when she had opened it, she saw the child: and, behold, the babe wept. And she had compassion on him, and said, This is one of the Hebrews' children.
7 Then said his sister to Pharaoh's daughter, Shall I go and call to thee a nurse of the Hebrew women, that she may nurse the child for thee?
8 And Pharaoh's daughter said to her, Go. And the maid went and called the child's mother.
9 And Pharaoh's daughter said unto her, Take this child away, and nurse it for me, and I will give thee thy wages. And the woman took the child, and nursed it.

Satan is attacking the Christian family through drugs, immorality, alcohol, music, and worldly lifestyles. These threats are part of a frontal attack, one that is directly aimed at destroying your child and home. We can thank the Lord for the protection He provides against these attacks! Just as He provided for Moses as he floated down the Nile, He wants to provide for us as we press forward on our journeys for the faith.

A. *He provided a place for Moses.*

God's grace is clearly seen throughout Moses' journey and specifically as God brings him to the palace to be cared for. Before the Egyptian princess thought to call for a nurse, God planned for Moses' own mother to raise him in the palace and provide a foundation of godliness. Many believe Jochebed was able to train and teach him until he was five or six years old.

In spite of the unusual circumstances, God allowed Moses' family to provide for him.

1 Timothy 5:8

8 But if any provide not for his own, and specially for those of his own house, he hath denied the faith, and is worse than an infidel.

God's unique provision prepared Moses for his future. Having the foundation of godliness instilled by his mother, Moses was then educated in Pharaoh's court. This gave him a knowledge of the inner workings of the palace, which he would later need as God's ambassador to that court.

B. He provides principles for us.

Ephesians 6:4

4 And, ye fathers, provoke not your children to wrath: but bring them up in the nurture and admonition of the Lord.

God commands us to train and teach our children.

Illustration

Often there is a gap between what is actually said and what the child hears. While teaching a group of children, a children's pastor was answering the question, "What is God like?" As he was explaining the eternality of God, he made this statement, "God is eternal." A young child quickly questioned what she heard. "God is a turtle?" she asked. She understood what was said in light of words familiar to her! We must remember to teach in ways that can be understood by a child!

God commands us to bring up our children in the nurture of the Lord. Nurture speaks of discipline. In

Lesson Three—The Journey to the Palace

1 Timothy 5:14, it is referred to as "guiding the house." *"I will therefore that the younger women marry, bear children,* **guide the house,** *give none occasion to the adversary to speak reproachfully."*

While many parents discipline out of a spirit of frustration and anger, may we exercise godliness and discipline our children from a heart of love.

We must also nurture in a home of order. Often, chaos and confusion can breed unruly children. May our homes be a place of loving correction and godly order as we seek to raise our children.

Raising godly children also requires admonition, which is teaching. Proverbs 1:8–9 say, *"My son, hear the instruction of thy father, and forsake not the law of thy mother: For they shall be an ornament of grace unto thy head, and chains about thy neck."*

May we never underestimate the importance of teaching. The choices young people make later in life will be greatly influenced by the protection and training they received in their early years.

Like Jochabed, may we purposefully teach our children on a daily basis. John Wesley, the great preacher of years gone by, said, "I learned more about God from my mother than from all the theologians in England."

Philippians 4:9

9   *Those things, which ye have both learned, and received, and heard, and seen in me, do: and the God of peace shall be with you.*

The greatest way to provide for your family is to pray that each one would know Jesus as his Saviour.

III. The Purpose of Moses

HEBREWS 11:24–26
24 By faith Moses, when he was come to years, refused to be called the son of Pharaoh's daughter;
25 Choosing rather to suffer affliction with the people of God, than to enjoy the pleasures of sin for a season;
26 Esteeming the reproach of Christ greater riches than the treasures in Egypt: for he had respect unto the recompense of the reward.

Like each one of us, God had a purpose for Moses. The purpose He had for Moses is the same purpose He has for us today. May we be challenged by the example of Moses, and be determined to fulfill God's purposes for our own lives.

A. *To identify with God's people*

Moses grew up to be a man who purposed to identify with God and his people. He refused to be called the son of Pharaoh's daughter, and in doing so, fulfilled God's purpose of identifying with Him.

God also commands this same identification from us. He desires that we identify and fellowship with God's people through the institution of the local church. Parents should become concerned when a teen is bent on acceptance from a peer or world system.

HEBREWS 10:25
25 Not forsaking the assembling of ourselves together, as the manner of some is; but exhorting one another: and so much the more, as ye see the day approaching.

B. To separate from sin

Illustration

A little boy was traveling with his mother over the holidays. As they approached the airline ticket counter the little guy informed the agent that he was two years old. Suspiciously, the agent looked down at the boy and asked, "Do you know what happens to little boys who lie?" The young traveler smiled, "Yep, they get to fly for half price!"

No matter how young or old we are, God desires that we separate from sin! Just as Daniel of the Old Testament, we must personally determine to separate from sin.

Daniel 1:8

8 But Daniel purposed in his heart that he would not defile himself with the portion of the king's meat, nor with the wine which he drank: therefore he requested of the prince of the eunuchs that he might not defile himself.

C. To wait on God's reward

The third purpose learned from the life of Moses is to wait on God's reward. God blesses those who follow Him on their journey. Earth's riches pale in comparison to the great rewards given by God.

Conclusion

Moses' journey for the faith was a journey of protection, provision and purpose. It is a journey on which God leads all of His children. May we rest in his protection, trust in His provision, and live out His purposes for our lives. May we protect, provide for, and give purpose to the next generation starting out on their journey for the faith.

Study Questions

1. Following Jochebed's example, from what two types of snares are we to protect our children?
   Children need to be protected from threats of evil and attacks from Satan.

2. Describe one way God has provided for you when you trusted Him.
   Answers will vary.

3. How is Satan attacking the Christian home today?
   Answers will vary, but should be in line with the following statement: Satan is attacking the Christian home by turning the hearts of the children away from their parents. He uses various methods to do this: television, friends, internet, music, and other wordly influences.

4. List the six ways we can protect our children.
   Give Warning
   Set Boundaries
   Set An Example
   Be Wise to That Which is Good
   Teach the Word of God
   Practice Forgiveness

5. According to Ephesians 6:4, how should we raise our children?
   We should bring them up in the nurture and admonition of the Lord.

Lesson Three—The Journey to the Palace

6. When it comes to identification, there is often a bent (in teens and adults alike) on acceptance from a peer or world system. List two sources from which you are tempted to seek acceptance (other than God and His people).
Answers will vary.

7. Using Hebrews 10:25 as a reference, identify one major way we can identify with God and His people.
We can identify with God and His people by being faithful in our church attendance.

Memory Verses

HEBREWS 11:24–26

24 By faith Moses, when he was come to years, refused to be called the son of Pharaoh's daughter;
25 Choosing rather to suffer affliction with the people of God, than to enjoy the pleasures of sin for a season;
26 Esteeming the reproach of Christ greater riches than the treasures in Egypt: for he had respect unto the recompense of the reward.

LESSON FOUR

The Journey to Egypt

Key Verses

Genesis 37:1–10

Lesson Overview

In this day of confusion, Christians must understand the truth of God's Word regarding the doctrine of salvation. It is vitally important to equip every saint with scriptural truths which can be used in witnessing to coworkers, friends, and relatives. Through study, Christians can prepare to answer people's questions about God's saving grace, using the authority of the Bible.

Salvation points to the core of God's love—the gift of His Son on the Cross. The truths in this lesson enable Christians to make a difference with their lives each day.

Lesson Aim

We want to impress upon the student the importance of faith, faithfulness, and forgiveness as key essentials to a successful journey.

Lesson Goals

At the conclusion of this lesson, students should:
- Strive to grow in their faith to receive God's commandments.
- Seek to grow in their faith to share God's Word with others.

- Desire to be faithful to God through burdens and blessings.
- Learn to forgive others, as Christ has forgiven us.
- Acknowledge God's eternal purpose in our lives.

Teaching Outline

I. A Journey of Faith
   A. Faith to receive God's revelation
   B. Faith to recite God's revelation

II. A Journey of Faithfulness
   A. When he was betrayed by his brethren
      1. They envied their brother.
      2. They persecuted their brother.
   B. When he was sold by his brethren
   C. When he was blessed in Egypt
   D. When he was unjustly accused
      1. Potiphar's wife attempted to seduce Joseph.
      2. Joseph was faithful to God.
      3. He was imprisoned for his faith.
      4. God's mercy sustained him.
      5. The Lord was with him.

III. A Journey of Forgiveness
   A. He forgave his brothers.
   B. He showed the grace of God.
   C. He showed the purpose of God.
   D. He focused on the Lord.
      1. He saw a heavenly perspective.
      2. He met an earthly need.

LESSON FOUR

The Journey to Egypt

Text

Genesis 37:1–10

Introduction

Horatio Nelson was a sickly boy living in eighteenth century England. As the nephew of a sea captain, he hoped one day to follow his uncle's example. Because Nelson's health was weak, his uncle was reluctant to take him on voyages. The death of his mother left him in the care of his uncle. Traveling on ship, he often became ill. His weak health finally forced Horatio to go home for a rest. Undaunted, he started another voyage as soon as possible. He was resolved to make his life worthy. He was promoted quickly to commander of a British ship, the *Agamemnon*. Commander Nelson fought in battle after battle, as he was always true to his mission in life—that his life should be worthy. Some sea battles were won; some were lost. During this time, he suffered much physical pain. He never flinched in the face of trouble. His strong resolve eventually made him a British hero. In a decisive battle, Lord Nelson led England to victory against Napoleon at Trafalgar. He was a man who was totally committed to his country. His determination made him unstoppable. Should Christians not be more committed to serve the one who gave His life to redeem us? What does it take to stop you from being faithful to God?

All people will face crisis at different times in their lives, and often, there are unexpected turns. Yet, I believe most people would want to say what the apostle Paul said at the end of his life:

2 Timothy 4:6–7

6 For I am now ready to be offered, and the time of my departure is at hand.
7 I have fought a good fight, I have finished my course, I have kept the faith:

Joseph was a man who finished his course. He was a man who suffered, yet he remained faithful to God. In many ways he was like the Lord Jesus Christ.

> Joseph was rejected by his brothers, so was Jesus.
> Joseph was loved by his father, so was Jesus.
> Joseph was victorious over temptation, so was Jesus.
> Joseph was taken into custody because of a false witness, so was Jesus.
> Joseph suffered from doing what was right, so did Jesus.
> Joseph was promoted from prison to rule the nation. Jesus was promoted from prison to rule the nations.

As we examine Joseph's journey, we admire his strength to remain faithful to God through the trials, temptations, and blessings that came into his life. He was a man who was greatly used by God, a true Bible hero. The secret of Joseph's strength of character was his unconditional faith in God. No matter what happened to him, his faith remained unshakable.

Let's notice Joseph's journey for God!

I. A Journey of Faith

Genesis 35:1–5

1 And God said unto Jacob, Arise, go up to Bethel, and dwell there: and make there an altar unto God, that appeared unto thee when thou fleddest from the face of Esau thy brother.
2 Then Jacob said unto his household, and to all that were with him, Put away the strange gods that are among you, and be clean, and change your garments:
3 And let us arise, and go up to Bethel; and I will make there an altar unto God, who answered me in the day of my distress, and was with me in the way which I went.
4 And they gave unto Jacob all the strange gods which were in their hand, and all their earrings which were in their ears; and Jacob hid them under the oak which was by Shechem.
5 And they journeyed: and the terror of God was upon the cities that were round about them, and they did not pursue after the sons of Jacob.

Faith is trusting in God's plan. Hebrews 11:6 says, *"But without faith it is impossible to please him: for he that cometh to God must believe that he is, and that he is a rewarder of them that diligently seek him."*

A. Faith to receive God's revelation
GENESIS 37:5
5 And Joseph dreamed a dream, and he told it his brethren: and they hated him yet the more.

God revealed his plan to Joseph in a dream, which gave him a glimpse of God's plan for his life. God revealed the time when Joseph would be a ruler and others would bow to him and that he would one day rule over his brothers.

Joseph's dream was of prophetic value. Dreams in ancient times were much attended to; hence, Joseph's dream, though he was a mere boy, engaged the serious consideration of his family.

It takes faith to receive and believe the truths found in the Word of God. But may we, like Joseph, exercise faith to receive God's Word and apply it to our lives.

1 THESSALONIANS 2:13
13 For this cause also thank we God without ceasing, because, when ye received the word of God which ye heard of us, ye received it not as the word of men, but as it is in truth, the word of God, which effectually worketh also in you that believe.

B. Faith to recite God's revelation
GENESIS 37:6–8
6 And he said unto them, Hear, I pray you, this dream which I have dreamed:

7 For, behold, we were binding sheaves in the field, and, lo, my sheaf arose, and also stood upright; and, behold, your sheaves stood round about, and made obeisance to my sheaf.

Lesson Four—The Journey to Egypt

8 And his brethren said to him, Shalt thou indeed reign over us? or shalt thou indeed have dominion over us? And they hated him yet the more for his dreams, and for his words.

Joseph acknowledged his revelation from God and had the faith to share it with his brothers. Resentment built in the hearts of his older brothers as Joseph recited the details of the dream to them.

First Thessalonians 2:4 says, *"But as we were allowed of God to be put in trust with the gospel, even so we **speak**; not as pleasing men, but God, which trieth our hearts."* Just as Joseph shared the news of his dream with his brothers, we must also be willing to speak—to share the Good News of the Gospel with those around us. It may not be easy. They may not happily receive you, but doing so pleases God and demonstrates our faith in Him.

His brothers did not like Joseph's dream, but it was not his dream; it was God's dream. Your neighbors may not like the Gospel message. But it's not your message, it's God's! This truth can bring great faith and confidence into the heart of the believer.

God had a special purpose for Joseph's life. Though He did not disclose every event along the journey, He promised to be with Joseph each step of the way.

Hebrews 13:5 says, *"Let your conversation be without covetousness; and be content with such things as ye have: for he hath said, I will never leave thee, nor forsake thee."* As God was with Joseph, so will He be with us on our journeys of faith. He knows what we need, and He will lovingly direct each step of the journey as we respond in faith.

II. A Journey of Faithfulness

1 Corinthians 4:2
2 Moreover it is required in stewards, that a man be found faithful.

Although no one plans for suffering, it is inevitable. When Joseph's journey brought him through times of despair, he simply remained faithful. When he was sold into slavery by his brothers, he remained steadfast. God took Joseph on a journey that at times seemed to be headed in the opposite direction of his expected end, but he continued to trust God.

Though Joseph could have quit many times, he never doubted. He never wavered even when circumstances seemed to destroy his dream. He kept doing what he knew God wanted him to do, and each trial strengthened his faith. Every experience prepared Joseph to fulfill God's purpose for his life.

A. *When he was betrayed by his brethren*

Joseph's brothers envied him, yet he remained faithful.

Genesis 37:11
11 And his brethren envied him; but his father observed the saying.

Joseph's brothers persecuted him and planned to kill him, but instead cast him into a pit. Through all of this, Joseph remained faithful. We do not read of him retaliating or getting even. He chose to trust God.

Genesis 37:20
20 Come now therefore, and let us slay him, and cast him into some pit, and we will say, Some evil beast hath

devoured him: and we shall see what will become of his dreams.

Each of us will experience seasons of opposition in our lives, but we must remember that God is always in control. We can learn from Joseph's brothers that God plans even our enemies! Your enemies may envy you and persecute you through gossip or slander, yet they are serving God's purpose in your life! God can use the trying circumstances in ways you wouldn't even imagine.

B. When he was sold by his brethren

GENESIS 37:27–28
27 Come, and let us sell him to the Ishmeelites, and let not our hand be upon him; for he is our brother and our flesh. And his brethren were content.
28 Then there passed by Midianites merchantmen; and they drew and lifted up Joseph out of the pit, and sold Joseph to the Ishmeelites for twenty pieces of silver: and they brought Joseph into Egypt.

Jealousy and envy developed in the hearts of Joseph's brothers who betrayed him and sold him into slavery, telling Jacob, their father, that Joseph was dead. (Do you ever feel your family or friends don't appreciate you? Remember Joseph!)

2 TIMOTHY 3:12
12 Yea, and all that will live godly in Christ Jesus shall suffer persecution.

It is required of a man that he be faithful, not successful. Looking back at the story of Joseph, being sold into slavery seemed to be the opposite of success and the opposite of God's plan for him. What looked like an unchangeable tragedy was another step in God's journey. Joseph's faith never wavered. He knew God was in control. God was the planner; Joseph was only the instrument in God's hands.

C. When he was blessed in Egypt
GENESIS 39:2
2   And the LORD was with Joseph, and he was a prosperous man; and he was in the house of his master the Egyptian.

Joseph continued to remain faithful through manifold suffering. He was betrayed by his brothers, sold into slavery, accused wrongly, and imprisoned unjustly. Nevertheless, through each circumstance, Joseph's faith was strengthened, and God blessed him on his journey. "But the God of all grace, who hath called us unto his eternal glory by Christ Jesus, after that ye have suffered a while, make you perfect, stablish, strengthen, settle you" (1 Peter 5:10).

God formed Joseph's life and found him faithful through trials and testing. Perhaps the greatest test Joseph would face was being exalted. Notice Pharaoh's accolades of Joseph:

GENESIS 41:39–40
39   And Pharaoh said unto Joseph, Forasmuch as God hath shewed thee all this, there is none so discreet and wise as thou art:
40   Thou shalt be over my house, and according unto thy word shall all my people be ruled: only in the throne will I be greater than thou.

Lesson Four—The Journey to Egypt

To some, being made a ruler in Egypt would be a dream come true. In reality, Joseph was called to occupy a position that was difficult and heavily laden with responsibility. Being second only to the ruler of Egypt brought a new temptation. While some may boast and take credit for their achievements, Joseph did not. He realized God had raised him up. *"But God is the judge: he putteth down one, and setteth up another"* (Psalm 75:7). To remain faithful and dependent on God was a great challenge. Joseph remained steadfast in his faith. He never forgot who blessed him; therefore, God blessed everything that he did.

Illustration

Lee Iacocca, the legendary carmaker, wrote in his autobiography: "Here I am in the twilight years of my life, still wondering what it's all about. I can tell you this: fame and fortune is for the birds."

D. *When he was unjustly accused*
Genesis 39:7–9
7 And it came to pass after these things, that his master's wife cast her eyes upon Joseph; and she said, Lie with me.
8 But he refused, and said unto his master's wife, Behold, my master wotteth not what is with me in the house, and he hath committed all that he hath to my hand;
9 There is none greater in this house than I; neither hath he kept back any thing from me but thee, because thou art his wife: how then can I do this great wickedness, and sin against God?

1. Potiphar's wife attempted to seduce Joseph.

Again, in a response indicative of his faithfulness to God, he refused the temptation. Joseph was willing to lose a coveted position in the world in order to maintain his integrity.

2 TIMOTHY 2:22

22 Flee also youthful lusts: but follow righteousness, faith, charity, peace, with them that call on the Lord out of a pure heart.

    Temptations will come, and they take many different forms. A believer who is faithful to God will strive to remain a clean vessel for His use. Today, as in Joseph's day, a person who wants to serve God must guard against choosing wrong when tempted. Satan will try any method to derail you from God's purpose for your life. Maintain your integrity.

    Choose to follow God and stay pure.

JAMES 1:12

12 Blessed is the man that endureth temptation: for when he is tried, he shall receive the crown of life, which the Lord hath promised to them that love him.

2. Joseph was faithful to God.

Someone said, "Joseph lost his coat, but he kept his character."

    Another person stated, "Character isn't created in a crisis, it only comes to light then."

Joseph and follow the pattern of Jesus Christ as we strive to forgive others on our journeys.

According to Joseph's original dream, his brethren had come to him for help. They had come to Egypt twice for food. The first time, Joseph recognized his brothers at once. They, however, could not recognize a brother who had not been seen for twenty years and had risen to be a great leader.

On their first encounter, Joseph acted as a foreigner. He kept Simeon and sent the other brothers on their way with instructions to return with Benjamin. Then, they returned a second time. Notice Joseph's response…

A. *He forgave his brothers.*
GENESIS 45:1–5
1 Then Joseph could not refrain himself before all them that stood by him; and he cried, Cause every man to go out from me. And there stood no man with him, while Joseph made himself known unto his brethren.
2 And he wept aloud: and the Egyptians and the house of Pharaoh heard.
3 And Joseph said unto his brethren, I am Joseph; doth my father yet live? And his brethren could not answer him; for they were troubled at his presence.
4 And Joseph said unto his brethren, Come near to me, I pray you. And they came near. And he said, I am Joseph your brother, whom ye sold into Egypt.
5 Now therefore be not grieved, nor angry with yourselves, that ye sold me hither: for God did send me before you to preserve life.

Joseph realized that God had used all the incidents in his life to bring him to this place of honor and did not take offense for the wounds his brothers had inflicted.

Instead, he realized that it was all a part of God's amazing plan. He forgave his brothers completely!

Illustration

Clara Barton, founder of the American Red Cross, was reminded one day of a vicious deed that someone had done to her years before. But she acted as if she had never even heard of the incident. "Don't you remember it?" her friend asked. "No," came Barton's reply, "I distinctly remember forgetting it." God is eager to forgive us!

1 JOHN 1:9
9 *If we confess our sins, he is faithful and just to forgive us our sins, and to cleanse us from all unrighteousness.*

EPHESIANS 4:32
32 *And be ye kind one to another, tenderhearted, forgiving one another, even as God for Christ's sake hath forgiven you.*

Even as Joseph was rejected by his own, Jesus Christ, who came nearly two thousand years later, was rejected by His own, and was crucified on the Cross. He offers salvation and forgiveness to all who believe. As Christ has so mercifully forgiven us, may we learn to forgive others!

B. He showed the grace of God.

The first time his brethren came, he placed their money back in the sacks.

GENESIS 42:25
25 *Then Joseph commanded to fill their sacks with corn, and to restore every man's money into his sack, and to give them provision for the way: and thus did he unto them.*

C. He showed the purpose of God.

GENESIS 45:7
7 And God sent me before you to preserve you a posterity in the earth, and to save your lives by a great deliverance.

Just like Joseph and his brothers, your circumstances are directed by God. He has an eternal purpose for each step of your journey. The Bible says, *"The steps of a good man are ordered by the LORD: and he delighteth in his way"* (Psalm 37:23). May we allow God to fulfill his purposes by taking each step as He orders it and by trusting Him along the way.

ROMANS 8:28
28 And we know that all things work together for good to them that love God, to them who are the called according to his purpose.

D. He focused on the Lord.
After Jacob died, the brothers thought Joseph would take revenge on them. Instead, Joseph focused on the Lord and His purposes.

GENESIS 50:19–21
19 And Joseph said unto them, Fear not: for am I in the place of God?
20 But as for you, ye thought evil against me; but God meant it unto good, to bring to pass, as it is this day, to save much people alive.
21 Now therefore fear ye not: I will nourish you, and your little ones. And he comforted them, and spake kindly unto them.

Joseph saw a heavenly perspective—God meant it for good. Do you see earthly situations from a heavenly perspective? Interruptions of our plans are divine appointments. Learn to see God as the one in control. Learn to see His hand in every situation.

Joseph also met an earthly need—He comforted his brothers and spake kindly to them. When we focus on the Lord, our actions will be Christ-like and Christ honoring.

As we walk on our journeys of faith, may we learn to focus on the Lord, just as Joseph did!

Conclusion

Joseph's journey to Egypt was unplanned, but it was all according to God's plan!

Joseph is an example to us of the steadfast commitment we should have as Christians.

At the end of his journey for the faith, Joseph was at all times found faithful. His journey may not have gone according to his plans, but it went according to God's plans. His life brought delight and honor to God as a result.

Lesson Four—The Journey to Egypt

Study Questions

1. Joseph had faith to accept God's Word in the form of a dream. Today, God's Word is given to us in the Bible. Is there a command or truth that you are struggling to receive? Take a moment and write a prayer to the Lord, sincerely communicating your desire to accept and receive His direction in your life.
   Answers will vary.

2. Joseph exercised faith to share God's Word with others. On a scale from 1–10, rate your personal soulwinning efforts. Now, create a brief action plan that will help increase your faith and efforts toward sharing the Gospel with others.
   Answers will vary, but a good action plan may include the following:
   Ask God to increase my faith.
   Go soulwinning at a specific time.
   Enlist a soulwinning partner.
   Keep record of personal prospects.

3. Name two things Joseph's brothers did to him.
   Joseph's brothers betrayed him and sold him into slavery.

4. According to 1 Corinthians 4:2, what is the one thing God requires of His stewards?
   God requires faithfulness of His stewards.

5. How could a promotion (to second-in-command over Egypt) have tempted Joseph to waver in his faithfulness to the Lord?
   Answers may vary, but should be similar to the following:

Blessings and promotions could have tempted Joseph to boast or take credit in his achievements, resulting in a failure to acknowledge God's working in his life. Ambition could have ruined him and his people.

6. How did Joseph show his forgiveness to his brothers?
   Joseph demonstrated his forgiveness by showing grace to his brothers and by focusing on God's eternal purpose.

7. According to Genesis 42:25, how did Joseph show grace to his brothers?
   He put money in their sacks.

8. How did Joseph demonstrate his focus on the Lord?
   He saw his situation from a heavenly perspective, and he met an earthly need.

Memory Verse

1 CORINTHIANS 15:58
58 *Therefore, my beloved brethren, be ye stedfast, unmoveable, always abounding in the work of the Lord, forasmuch as ye know that your labour is not in vain in the Lord.*

LESSON FIVE

The Journey to Sinai

Text

Exodus 31:18–32:6, 30–33

Introduction

The ten Boom family were devout Christians. Their home was used by the Haarlem, Holland Underground as a hiding place during the Nazi occupation. Many of the people staying there in 1944 were hidden illegally while they were waiting for another safe house to be located. Through the ten Boom's activities as part of the Haarlem Underground, they and their friends saved the lives of an estimated eight hundred Jews.

On February 28, 1944, the family was betrayed and the Nazi secret police raided their home arresting Corrie and other members of her family. Some were killed and others were sent to the death camps. Corrie and her sister, Betsie, were sent to Ravensbruck Concentration Camp. Life was almost unbearable, but the sisters spent their time witnessing about their God, sharing the faith that was evident in their lives. At times, it must have seemed as though God was not hearing their prayers while in the prison. A quotation was found on the wall of one of the prisons. It read:

> I believe in love when the world is full of hate.
> I believe in the sun even when it is not shining.
> I believe in God even when He is silent.

Ultimately, four of the ten Booms gave their lives for their commitment to hiding the Jews. Corrie realized that her life was a gift from God. She spent the last years of her life sharing what she had learned with others all over the world.

The life of Corrie ten Boom provides a wonderful example of waiting on God. She trusted Him and waited patiently to see how He would work on her behalf and direct her on her journey. Unlike Corrie ten Boom, the children of Israel came to a point where they refused to wait on God during their journey for the faith.

In Exodus, we see the mighty hand of God in bringing His children out of Egypt.

God brought the plagues to Egypt through Moses.

The Israelites were let go and were free for the first time in four hundred years.

God opened the Red Sea to deliver Israel from the Egyptian army and drowned the army at the same time.

God provided the daily food of manna.

A few weeks into this historical journey, God called Moses to a special and historic meeting at Mt. Sinai. On this particular journey, Moses received the Ten Commandments, which would be the cornerstone of the law.

Decalogue (noun)
Ten Commandments

God demonstrated His care for the children of Israel time after time. He was taking them on a long journey to strengthen their faith. He would prove Himself strong repeatedly on their behalf.

I. A Glorious Journey

Exodus 31:18
18 And he gave unto Moses, when he had made an end of communing with him upon mount Sinai, two tables of testimony, tables of stone, written with the finger of God.

Moses was God's chosen leader for Israel. His life had been directed by God since birth. His mother Jochebed trusted God to protect her son from the evil edict of the Pharaoh. From his childhood in the palace to God's chosen leader, Moses' journey was an example of a man who was a friend of God.

Deuteronomy 34:10
10 And there arose not a prophet since in Israel like unto Moses, whom the Lord knew face to face,

Through his faithfulness, Moses had merited the privilege to speak to God as His friend. Exodus 33:11 says, "*And the Lord spake unto Moses face to face, as a man speaketh unto his friend....*" God desires our communion with Him to be as friend to friend.

Moses was a man favored in the eyes of the Lord. Exodus 33:17 says, "*And the Lord said unto Moses, I will do this thing also that thou hast spoken: for thou hast found grace in my sight, and I know thee by name.*" He continually sought to obey and honor God with his life.

God led Moses and Israel to this point in their journey and was preparing to hand them the greatest Law book in history.

A. The reunion

In Exodus 31:18, we see the unique reunion of God and Moses. This special relationship began when Moses came to the burning bush and communed with God for the first time.

Exodus 3:4

4 *And when the* Lord *saw that he turned aside to see, God called unto him out of the midst of the bush, and said, Moses, Moses. And he said, Here am I.*

> **Communing** (verb)
> to speak; to promise

In Exodus 31, we learn that Moses had been communing with the Lord for forty days without food or water. He was so occupied with the Lord that even the very basics of life were ignored.

Deuteronomy 9:9–11

9 *When I was gone up into the mount to receive the tables of stone, even the tables of the covenant which the* Lord *made with you, then I abode in the mount forty days and forty nights, I neither did eat bread nor drink water:*
10 *And the* Lord *delivered unto me two tables of stone written with the finger of God; and on them was written according to all the words, which the* Lord *spake with you in the mount out of the midst of the fire in the day of the assembly.*
11 *And it came to pass at the end of forty days and forty nights, that the* Lord *gave me the two tables of stone, even the tables of the covenant.*

B. The revelation

The information God gave to Moses was so important that He wrote it with His own fingers and gave it directly to Moses to give to the people.

Revelation is truth given from God to man that was not previously known nor could be known except when God gave it. God spoke to the children of Israel through Moses. And, when God delivered his people from the bondage in Egypt, He revealed Himself through His righteous acts toward them.

> **Revelation** (noun)
> the act of God revealing truths to humans that they would otherwise not know

Today we have the Bible, God's complete revelation to us. It is a book about God. It recounts His active participation in the lives of people and their response to Him. The Bible tells us how to walk on our journeys of faith, and it reveals God's dealings with men as examples to us.

The Bible illustrates God's wisdom, love, power, and glory. It reveals the holy nature of God to us through His actions and His words. God's Word, the Bible, is the only book given to us by God. It is inspired; it is true and inerrant. It is His revelation to us.

TEACHING TIP

The biblical description of God writing with His finger would be what is referred to as "anthropomorphism" which simply means that God is described as having human-like qualities such as having human form.

2 Peter 1:21

21 For the prophecy came not in old time by the will of man: but holy men of God spake as they were moved by the Holy Ghost.

Psalm 119:160

160 Thy word is true from the beginning: and every one of thy righteous judgments endureth for ever.

God spoke to the children of Israel through His servant Moses. Today, God expresses His will to us through the Bible. May we never lose sight of this glorious truth and privilege—God has revealed Himself to us through His Word!

Hebrews 1:1–2

1 God, who at sundry times and in divers manners spake in time past unto the fathers by the prophets,
2 Hath in these last days spoken unto us by his Son, whom he hath appointed heir of all things, by whom also he made the worlds;

II. A Grievous Juncture

Exodus 32:1–6

1 And when the people saw that Moses delayed to come down out of the mount, the people gathered themselves together unto Aaron, and said unto him, Up, make us gods, which shall go before us; for as for this Moses, the man that brought us up out of the land of Egypt, we wot not what is become of him.
2 And Aaron said unto them, Break off the golden earrings, which are in the ears of your wives, of your sons, and of your daughters, and bring them unto me.

Many people today waste and misuse what God has given to them. What is meant to be used for God's glory is used for personal pleasure. People give their talents to the world, their money to worldly vice, and their opportunities to personal advancement. Many people take their God-given possessions (whether material or physical) and create modern-day idols, allowing an object or an idea to take the place of God in their hearts.

May we be a people free of idolatry as we travel on our journeys of faith, and may we worship God His way from a pure heart!

In verses 5–6, we see the carousing of the people. They rose up early, brought offerings, ate, drank, and played. They were so loud that Joshua heard the noise and thought war was breaking out in the camp!

Exodus 32:17–18
17 And when Joshua heard the noise of the people as they shouted, he said unto Moses, There is a noise of war in the camp.
18 And he said, It is not the voice of them that shout for mastery, neither is it the voice of them that cry for being overcome: but the noise of them that sing do I hear.

Exodus 32:5 gives record of Aaron's proclamation. He declared the next day to be a feast unto the Lord. He was trying to point people to the true God, using Egyptian methods. The formal system of worship that God was giving to Moses was not yet established. So, it is possible that Aaron's intention was right, but the method he used was wrong.

1 Corinthians 10:21–22

21 Ye cannot drink the cup of the Lord, and the cup of devils: ye cannot be partakers of the Lord's table, and of the table of devils.

22 Do we provoke the Lord to jealousy? are we stronger than he?

2 Corinthians 6:15–17

15 And what concord hath Christ with Belial? or what part hath he that believeth with an infidel?

16 And what agreement hath the temple of God with idols? for ye are the temple of the living God; as God hath said, I will dwell in them, and walk in them; and I will be their God, and they shall be my people.

17 Wherefore come out from among them, and be ye separate, saith the Lord, and touch not the unclean thing; and I will receive you,

In Exodus 32:6, we see the people's actions. They did rise up early and brought offerings, performing some spiritual actions; however, it only got worse from there.

Exodus 32:6

6 And they rose up early on the morrow, and offered burnt offerings, and brought peace offerings; and the people sat down to eat and to drink, and rose up to play.

Illustration

Narcissism is a growing concern in American culture. A new comprehensive study on the subject was released in February 2007. Five psychologists, who are worried about the negative effect self-absorption is having on personal relationships and society at large, examined the results of over 16,000 college students. They noted a steady increase in scores that reflect an unhealthy disposition toward narcissistic behavior. Dr. Twenge says, "Current technology fuels the increase in narcissism. By its very name, MySpace encourages attention-seeking, as does YouTube." She even noted that volunteerism among young people can be self-serving in that it is needed for college applications and career advancement. Keith Campbell, co-author of the study, voiced concerns about relational fallout. He said the study asserts that narcissists "are more likely to have romantic relationships that are short-lived, at risk for infidelity, lack emotional warmth, and to exhibit game-playing, dishonesty, and over controlling and violent behaviors." Twenge affirmed that narcissists tend to lack empathy, react aggressively to criticism and favor self-promotion instead of helping others.

narcissism (noun) fascination with oneself; vanity; excessive self-love

It appears the children of Israel went much further than simply performing spiritual actions, for the Bible says they "rose up to play," a phrase which seems to imply fornication and adultery. In some countries the verb "to play" is still used precisely in this sense. How sad that their idolatrous hearts took them this far into sin.

1 Corinthians 10:6–7

6   Now these things were our examples, to the intent we should not lust after evil things, as they also lusted.
7   Neither be ye idolaters, as were some of them; as it is written, The people sat down to eat and drink, and rose up to play.

rose up to play (verb) to laugh, mock, play, to jest, to sport, play, make sport, toy with, make a toy of

> **Quote**
>
> May the church always be a holy place of worship, not a playhouse for immature believers.
>
> Are you at a grievous juncture? Does your life show indications of an impatient or idolatrous heart? Take inventory of your life today and be willing to come to God for cleansing and forgiveness, if necessary.

III. A Gracious Judgment

EXODUS 32:30–33

30 And it came to pass on the morrow, that Moses said unto the people, Ye have sinned a great sin: and now I will go up unto the Lord; peradventure I shall make an atonement for your sin.

31 And Moses returned unto the Lord, and said, Oh, this people have sinned a great sin, and have made them gods of gold.

32 Yet now, if thou wilt forgive their sin—; and if not, blot me, I pray thee, out of thy book which thou hast written.

33 And the Lord said unto Moses, Whosoever hath sinned against me, him will I blot out of my book.

> **atonement** (noun)
> to cover, purge, make an atonement, make reconciliation, to cover over, pacify, propitiate- to cover over, atone for sin, make atonement for

A. *The prayer of Moses*

The prayer of Moses is recorded in verses 30–33 of our text. He intercedes for the people and pleads on their behalf.

The reference to "thy book" is the first Biblical reference made regarding names being recorded in a book. The book referred to in our passage may not be the actual "Book of Life" later mentioned in the Scriptures, but rather a record of all the families and tribes of Israel. Perhaps because they disobeyed the Lord, they would have not been allowed to enter the Promised Land. Moses may have been requesting that if the people would be forbidden to enter the Promised Land, he would want his name blotted out of the book, as well. This is certainly a picture of the future when God will open the Book of Life and only those whose names appear in that book will enter into the eternal inheritance.

Philippians 4:3
3 And I intreat thee also, true yokefellow, help those women which laboured with me in the gospel, with Clement also, and with other my fellowlabourers, whose names are in the book of life.

Revelations 20:12–15
12 And I saw the dead, small and great, stand before God; and the books were opened: and another book was opened, which is the book of life: and the dead were judged out of those things which were written in the books, according to their works.
13 And the sea gave up the dead which were in it; and death and hell delivered up the dead which were in them: and they were judged every man according to their works.
14 And death and hell were cast into the lake of fire. This is the second death.
15 And whosoever was not found written in the book of life was cast into the lake of fire.

B. The problem of Moses

Moses had a problem in that he could not save the people whose names were being blotted out of the book.

No man can offer reconciliation; it comes only through Jesus Christ.

Hebrews 10:9–14

9 Then said he, Lo, I come to do thy will, O God. He taketh away the first, that he may establish the second.
10 By the which will we are sanctified through the offering of the body of Jesus Christ once for all.
11 And every priest standeth daily ministering and offering oftentimes the same sacrifices, which can never take away sins:
12 But this man, after he had offered one sacrifice for sins for ever, sat down on the right hand of God;
13 From henceforth expecting till his enemies be made his footstool.
14 For by one offering he hath perfected for ever them that are sanctified.

We all have this same problem: we cannot save ourselves or reconcile ourselves to God. Just as Moses could not save the children of Israel, no priest or man can offer salvation to us. We must come to Jesus in faith, believing that He will save us from our sins. If this is something you have not done, settle it today! If you have been reconciled to God, thank Him for your salvation and for the assurance of the fact that your name is recorded in the Book of Life!

Conclusion

While Moses was enjoying a glorious encounter with God Himself, the children of Israel were at a grievous juncture, impatiently choosing to worship God their own way. As a result of their disobedience, God offered gracious judgment to the children of Israel. As we go through our week, may we remember the goodness of God in offering salvation, and may we share this good news with others!

Acts 4:12

12 *Neither is there salvation in any other: for there is none other name under heaven given among men, whereby we must be saved.*

Study Questions

1. According to Exodus 3:4, when did God commune with Moses for the first time?
   God communed with Moses for the first time at the burning bush.

2. Look up Deuteronomy 34:10 and Exodus 33:11. Describe the relationship between God and Moses.
   They spoke face to face, as a man speaks to his friend. These verses suggest that Moses had nothing to hide from God. He communed closely with Him.

3. Moses communed with God for forty days and nights without interruption. How is your communion with God? List three steps you can take this week to improve your relationship with God.
   Answers will vary, but may include the following:
   Get up earlier to spend more time in Bible reading.
   Designate a specific time and place to spend time with God each day.
   Keep a journal of prayers and answers to prayer.

4. List the two indications that the children of Israel had come to a grievous juncture on their journey.
   The children of Israel had become idolatrous and impatient.

5. An idol is something that takes God's place in your heart. In the space provided, identify a potential idol in your life; then pause to pray that God will keep your heart free of idolatry on your journey for the faith.
   Answers will vary.

6. What was Moses' problem, as recorded in the Scripture (Exodus 32:30–33) and how is it similar to the problem mankind faces today?
Moses could not save himself or the children of Israel, and we cannot save ourselves or others. We are saved by faith in God alone.

Memory Verse

2 Corinthians 6:16

16 And what agreement hath the temple of God with idols? for ye are the temple of the living God; as God hath said, I will dwell in them, and walk in them; and I will be their God, and they shall be my people.

LESSON SIX

The Journey to the Promised Land

Key Verses

Joshua 1:1–9

Lesson Overview

Moses, the leader of Israel had died. Joshua, God's chosen leader had taken his place. He was the man who would lead the children of Israel into the Promised Land. We will study the life of Joshua and discover why God chose him to lead the children of Israel.

Lesson Aim

Many Christians feel inadequate when called upon by God to lead. God gives us the example of Joshua as he is placed in a position of leadership. We will look at how God prepared him and supplied everything he needed to do what God wanted him to do.

Lesson Goals

At the conclusion of this lesson, students should:
- Recognize the character traits in Joshua's life that made him a leader God could use.
- Realize that God calls every Christian to some measure of influence and leadership.
- Understand the responsibilities that come with God-given influence.

- Claim the resources God offers to those who seek to be used of Him.

Teaching Outline

I. Joshua's Resume
   A. He was proven.
   B. He was a servant.
   C. He was patient.
   D. He had a vision.

II. Joshua's Responsibility
   A. To provide leadership
      1. He leads his family.
      2. He leads the people.
   B. To claim the promises
      1. To claim the land
      2. To conquer the enemy

III. Joshua's Resources
   A. God's presence
   B. God's preserved Word

LESSON SIX

The Journey to the Promised Land

Text

Joshua 1:1–9

Introduction

Amid the indifference to missions in nineteenth century England, one man's efforts stand out. A cobbler by trade, William also pastored a small Baptist congregation. He was consumed with bringing the Gospel to the peoples of the world. One day in the quietness of his cobbler shop, he surrendered to God's call to the mission field. Believing it was the duty of every man who believed the Gospel to make it known throughout the world, he said, "Here am I; send me."

Through ridicule and rejection, sacrifice and suffering, William persisted. He knew that God wanted to use him to reach people of all nations. Though there were no mission boards and there was no real interest in sending missionaries, he persisted in fulfilling his call. Through one sermon preached throughout England entitled, "Expect Great Things from God, Attempt Great Things for God," a missionary society was begun.

William finally reached India where he ministered faithfully for seven years before he saw one Indian salvation. Amid disease, death, and discouragement in both reaching his mission field and serving there, one characteristic of his life stands out; he kept his focus on God, and God gave him the grace to continue. William was God's instrument to awaken England to the command to evangelize the world. Near the end of his life, William called out to a missionary friend, "You have been speaking about Dr. Carey. When I am gone, say nothing about Dr. Carey—speak about Dr. Carey's God."

Just as William Carey found himself at a crossroads—a point where he had to choose between serving God as a missionary or staying in England—we, too, often come to crossroads in our lives. We come to points of decision where we must take action. At those points of decision, it is determined whether or not we will do something great for God.

1 KINGS 18:21

21 And Elijah came unto all the people, and said, How long halt ye between two opinions? if the LORD be God, follow him: but if Baal, then follow him. And the people answered him not a word.

In Joshua 1, we find the children of Israel at a crossroads. Moses had been God's chosen leader from the time of their deliverance from Egypt, through their wandering in wilderness, and right up to the boundary of the Promised Land. There Moses, the servant of the Lord, died. Their leader was gone, and they were at a point of decision. Would the children of Israel finally claim the promises of God and enter the land or would they turn back to the ways of Egypt?

Though the circumstances seemed bleak, God had a plan for this moment of decision! He wanted His people to claim His promises. So, He chose a man to lead His people. (God will always use this method to accomplish His purposes. God chooses men to lead His people.)

God chose Joshua as the new leader of Israel. Joshua had been a servant to Moses. He was trained by Moses and would lead with the same purpose and carry on the same work. Even though Moses was dead, God's plan for Israel was still alive.

DEUTERONOMY 34:9

9 *And Joshua the son of Nun was full of the spirit of wisdom; for Moses had laid his hands upon him: and the children of Israel hearkened unto him, and did as the LORD commanded Moses.*

I. Joshua's Resume

Joshua demonstrated a strong faith during his journey. Yet, leading the children of Israel to possess the land was a tremendous task that would require perhaps an even greater faith. Looking at the circumstances, Joshua must have known they could not conquer this challenge in their own strength. However, he was confident in God's promise that He would be with him and they would possess the land.

JOSHUA 1:2–5

2 *Moses my servant is dead; now therefore arise, go over this Jordan, thou, and all this people, unto the land which I do give to them, even to the children of Israel.*

3 *Every place that the sole of your foot shall tread upon, that have I given unto you, as I said unto Moses.*

4 From the wilderness and this Lebanon even unto the great river, the river Euphrates, all the land of the Hittites, and unto the great sea toward the going down of the sun, shall be your coast.

5 There shall not any man be able to stand before thee all the days of thy life: as I was with Moses, so I will be with thee: I will not fail thee, nor forsake thee.

Some may wonder, *Why was Joshua able to enter the Promised Land when so many from his generation were unable?* Joshua was used of God and was able to enter the Promised Land because he was a man of great character. Notice Joshua's resume.

Psalm 75:6–7

6 For promotion cometh neither from the east, nor from the west, nor from the south,

7 But God is the judge: he putteth down one, and setteth up another.

A. He was proven.

After God provided water from the rock at Horeb, Amalek came and fought with Israel. During this battle, Joshua proved himself to be obedient, courageous, and trustworthy. He did what Moses commanded him to do and "discomfited" Amalek and his people.

Exodus 17:8–13

8 Then came Amalek, and fought with Israel in Rephidim.

9 And Moses said unto Joshua, Choose us out men, and go out, fight with Amalek: to morrow I will stand on the top of the hill with the rod of God in mine hand.

10 So Joshua did as Moses had said to him, and fought with Amalek: and Moses, Aaron, and Hur went up to the top of the hill.

11 And it came to pass, when Moses held up his hand, that Israel prevailed: and when he let down his hand, Amalek prevailed.

12 But Moses' hands were heavy; and they took a stone, and put it under him, and he sat thereon; and Aaron and Hur stayed up his hands, the one on the one side, and the other on the other side; and his hands were steady until the going down of the sun.

13 And Joshua discomfited Amalek and his people with the edge of the sword.

Joshua demonstrated great faith as he fought against the Amalekites, and in doing so, proved himself to be someone who could be used of God.

Quote

A faith that is not worth testing is not worth trusting.

B. He was a servant.

When people today use the term *servant*, it many times suggests a position of low esteem. Yet, when God uses the term servant, it signifies honor and greatness. In the Bible, God often referred to His chosen leaders as servants.

Exodus 24:12–13

12 And the LORD said unto Moses, Come up to me into the mount, and be there: and I will give thee tables of stone, and a law, and commandments which I have written; that thou mayest teach them.

13 And Moses rose up, and his minister Joshua: and Moses went up into the mount of God.

Mark 10:45
45 For even the Son of man came not to be ministered unto, but to minister, and to give his life a ransom for many.

Joshua was a servant to Moses. We see this specifically demonstrated while Moses was on Mt. Sinai receiving the Ten Commandments. While Moses was on the mountain for forty days and nights, Joshua patiently waited for him and ministered to him.

People are prepared to lead when they have learned to serve. Joshua learned to serve before God made him a leader.

Joshua not only learned to serve God, but he also learned to serve men. He was not less of a leader because he served others. Serving God and others was the overshadowing purpose for all of his actions.

Quote

The measure of a man's greatness is not how many people serve him, but how many he serves.

Mark 10:43–44
43 But so shall it not be among you: but whosoever will be great among you, shall be your minister:
44 And whosoever of you will be the chiefest, shall be servant of all.

Galatians 5:13
13 For, brethren, ye have been called unto liberty; only use not liberty for an occasion to the flesh, but by love serve one another.

Lesson Six—The Journey to the Promised Land

When Joshua was chosen to be the leader of Israel, he was a servant to Moses. At the end of his life, Joshua was still known as a servant of the Lord. May we learn from his example and seek to be true and faithful servants of God!

Judges 2:8
8 And Joshua the son of Nun, the servant of the Lord, died, being an hundred and ten years old.

C. He was patient.

Exodus 24:18
18 And Moses went into the midst of the cloud, and gat him up into the mount. And Moses was in the mount forty days and forty nights.

Exodus 32:15–17
15 And Moses turned, and went down from the mount, and the two tables of the testimony were in his hand: the tables were written on both their sides; on the one side and on the other were they written.
16 And the tables were the work of God, and the writing was the writing of God, graven upon the tables.
17 And when Joshua heard the noise of the people as they shouted, he said unto Moses, There is a noise of war in the camp.

Joshua spent forty days waiting for Moses on Mount Sinai. He could have gotten impatient, frustrated, or bored, but he chose to faithfully and patiently anticipate Moses' needs.

Joshua's journey for the faith serves as an excellent example of patience! Many Christians today don't think twice before they resign from their class, bus route, or church. But, God desires that we remain patient on our journeys, trusting Him to accomplish His work in and through us.

Joshua's patience paid off when he received the blessing of entering the Promised Land. We too will be glad when we receive the blessings of patiently waiting on the Lord.

PSALM 27:14

14 Wait on the LORD: be of good courage, and he shall strengthen thine heart: wait, I say, on the LORD.

Illustration

During World War II, Hitler began to blitz London. The British government evacuated people by the train loads. As the citizens of England were running toward the trains, a man saw a young boy running to safety by himself. The man looked at the boy and said, "You know where you're going?" The boy replied, "No, but the king does!"

We may not know where God is taking us on our journeys of faith, and we may not understand periods of waiting and silence. But we can trust the heart and plan of our King and wait patiently on the Lord.

D. *He had a vision.*

NUMBERS 14:6–10

6 And Joshua the son of Nun, and Caleb the son of Jephunneh, which were of them that searched the land, rent their clothes:

7 And they spake unto all the company of the children of Israel, saying, The land, which we passed through to search it, is an exceeding good land.

Lesson Six—The Journey to the Promised Land

8 If the Lord delight in us, then he will bring us into this land, and give it us; a land which floweth with milk and honey.

9 Only rebel not ye against the Lord, neither fear ye the people of the land; for they are bread for us: their defence is departed from them, and the Lord is with us: fear them not.

10 But all the congregation bade stone them with stones. And the glory of the Lord appeared in the tabernacle of the congregation before all the children of Israel.

Joshua had a godly vision. When he and Caleb searched out the land God had promised to them, they came back excited and energized by what they saw. The land was exceedingly good, and it flowed with milk and honey!

Joshua's vision to claim the land was based upon God's words, and he never lost sight of it.

Joshua 1:6

6 Be strong and of a good courage: for unto this people shalt thou divide for an inheritance the land, which I sware unto their fathers to give them.

Joshua knew that the children of Israel would possess the Promised Land because God had promised it. He acted on his belief.

Proverbs 29:18

18 Where there is no vision, the people perish: but he that keepeth the law, happy is he.

II. Joshua's Responsibility

A. *To provide leadership*

On your journey for the faith, God will appoint you to a position of leadership. You may not even recognize it when He does! Leadership is influence; therefore we all lead because we all influence others. For some, it will be leading at home, in a classroom, or on a bus route. For others it will be leading a church or a business. No matter what capacity God has designed for us to fill, each one of us is called to be a leader.

Joshua provided great leadership for his family. We see this identified in Joshua 24:15.

JOSHUA 24:15

15 And if it seem evil unto you to serve the LORD, choose you this day whom ye will serve; whether the gods which your fathers served that were on the other side of the flood, or the gods of the Amorites, in whose land ye dwell: but as for me and my house, we will serve the LORD.

It is time for dads to take leadership in the home. Many times, a man may be a leader at his work, but he fails to be a leader in the home. Men must determine to lead their families in God's direction.

Illustration

Time Magazine: "Rising divorce rates and out-of-wedlock births mean that more than 40% of all children born between 1970 and 1984 are likely to spend much of their childhood living in single parent homes."

The impact of these fatherless homes on the children is significant, if not devastating.

Time goes on to say, "Studies of young criminals have found that more than 70% of all juveniles in state reform institutions come from fatherless homes. Children from broken families are nearly twice as likely as those in two-parent families to drop out of high school." (Time.com, June 16, 2007)

Joshua was a great leader because he first followed God's leading. Fathers must also follow God's leading in their lives and homes in order to be effective leaders for their families.

Joshua led his family, but he also led God's people.

JOSHUA 1:10
10 Then Joshua commanded the officers of the people, saying,

Joshua commanded the officers of the people. Perhaps it was difficult or uncomfortable to do so, but he was to lead that generation for the Lord!

Quote

"What is the difference between an obstacle and an opportunity? Our attitude toward it. Every opportunity has a difficulty, and every difficulty has an opportunity."
—J. SIDLOW BAXTER

B. To claim the promises

JOSHUA 1:4–5
4 From the wilderness and this Lebanon even unto the great river, the river Euphrates, all the land of the Hittites, and unto the great sea toward the going down of the sun, shall be your coast.

5 There shall not any man be able to stand before thee all the days of thy life: as I was with Moses, so I will be with thee: I will not fail thee, nor forsake thee.

Joshua had the great responsibility to claim the land God had promised to His people.

> **TEACHING TIP**
>
> *The Promised Land was 300,000 square miles*

Because of a lack of faith, Israel never claimed more than 10% of the land God had given to them. Sadly, this response to God's promises is typical of most Christians today. Perhaps there are some promises of God that you must take the responsibility to claim in your life!

JEREMIAH 29:11
11 For I know the thoughts that I think toward you, saith the LORD, thoughts of peace, and not of evil, to give you an expected end.

Often, God wants to bless us but does not because of our lack of faith. Perhaps you have memorized some Bible promises; do you have enough confidence in God to claim them? What is holding you back from going forward on your journey of faith? Until you act on God's promises, you will not experience victory.

Joshua also claimed God's promise that he would conquer his enemies.

JOSHUA 1:5A
5 There shall not any man be able to stand before thee all the days of thy life:

God promised Joshua complete victory in conquering the enemy. In the same way, He promises us complete victory over sin. He promises that we can be more than conquerors through Him! Thank God for this wonderful promise!

1 Corinthians 15:57
57 But thanks be to God, which giveth us the victory through our Lord Jesus Christ.

Romans 8:36–37
36 As it is written, For thy sake we are killed all the day long; we are accounted as sheep for the slaughter.
37 Nay, in all these things we are more than conquerors through him that loved us.

III. Joshua's Resources

Joshua 1:5b–8
5 ...as I was with Moses, so I will be with thee: I will not fail thee, nor forsake thee.
6 Be strong and of a good courage: for unto this people shalt thou divide for an inheritance the land, which I sware unto their fathers to give them.
7 Only be thou strong and very courageous, that thou mayest observe to do according to all the law, which Moses my servant commanded thee: turn not from it to the right hand or to the left, that thou mayest prosper whithersoever thou goest.
8 This book of the law shall not depart out of thy mouth; but thou shalt meditate therein day and night, that thou mayest observe to do according to all that is written therein: for then thou shalt make thy way prosperous, and then thou shalt have good success.

Have you ever started your day with the thought, *How will all this get done?* Perhaps that is how Joshua felt when he assumed leadership and began to claim God's promises. There was much work to be done in order to enjoy the victory of the Promised Land.

As God always does, He provided the resources Joshua needed to accomplish His Work. These resources are still available to us today; they are just as powerful and helpful as they were during the time of Joshua.

A. God's presence (v. 5)

HEBREWS 13:5–6

5 Let your conversation be without covetousness; and be content with such things as ye have: for he hath said, I will never leave thee, nor forsake thee.
6 So that we may boldly say, The Lord is my helper, and I will not fear what man shall do unto me.

ZECHARIAH 4:6

6 Then he answered and spake unto me, saying, This is the word of the LORD unto Zerubbabel, saying, Not by might, nor by power, but by my spirit, saith the LORD of hosts.

Illustration

The story is told of some preachers, who, many years ago, were discussing D.L. Moody and the possibility of inviting him to speak at one of their meetings. One of the preachers who opposed asking D.L. Moody, somewhat critically asked, "Does D.L. Moody have a monopoly on the Holy Spirit?" To which an older and wiser preacher replied, "No. The Holy Spirit has a monopoly on D.L. Moody."

God told Moses, *"Now therefore go and I will be with thy mouth…"* (Exodus 4:12).

God told Joshua, *"I will be with thee…"* (Joshua 1:5).

God told Jeremiah, *"And they shall fight against thee; but they shall not prevail against thee; for I am with thee, saith the Lord, to deliver thee"* (Jeremiah 1:19).

God says to us, *"Go ye therefore, and teach all nations, baptizing them in the name of the father, and of the Son, and of the Holy Ghost: Teaching them to observe all things whatsoever I have commanded you: and, lo, I am with you alway, even unto the end of the world"* (Matthew 28:19–20).

B. God's preserved Word (v. 8)

That same Book of the Law has been kept for us today. God has preserved the wonderful resource of His Word.

Matthew 5:18

18 For verily I say unto you, Till heaven and earth pass, one jot or one tittle shall in no wise pass from the law, till all be fulfilled.

God commanded Joshua to meditate on this resource, the Bible. How much time do you spend meditating in and thinking on God's Word?

Quote

If we want the God of truth we must know the truth of God!

God also commanded Joshua to obey His Word. He told him to observe *to do*, not just to simply observe!

People often mark their Bibles, but their Bibles don't mark them!

Paul exhorted us to let the Word of Christ dwell in us richly. Perhaps you are not using the resource of God's Word like you should. If not, decide today that you will use this wonderful resource on your journey.

Conclusion

Joshua was faithful to lead the people into the Promised Land. In what area is God leading you to provide leadership and make a difference?

Lesson Six—The Journey to the Promised Land

Study Questions

1. What character traits in Joshua's life should we seek to emulate?
   Joshua was a servant. He was proven and patient, and He had a God-given vision.

2. Take a moment to review Joshua's resume. Identify a characteristic in which you are weakest, and list an action that will help you strengthen your weakness in that area this week.
   Answers will vary as to personal experience.

3. Joshua had two major responsibilities given to him from the Lord. What were they?
   Joshua was to provide leadership and claim God's promises.

4. Identify a key area where you have a sphere of influence over others.
   Answers will vary, but may include the following: mother, father, teacher, babysitter, employee, friend, etc.

5. How is God using your life to influence others?
   Answers will vary as to personal experience.

6. What resources has God promised to give you on your journey of influence?
   God offers His promises and His presence.

7. God's Word is full of promises to the believer. Perhaps there is a certain promise that you have difficulty claiming. If so, list the promise below, and write out a

prayer to the Lord, telling him that you will claim His promise in your life.
Answers will vary as to personal experience.

Memory Verse

2 Peter 3:18

18 But grow in grace, and in the knowledge of our Lord and Saviour Jesus Christ. To him be glory both now and for ever. Amen.

LESSON SEVEN

The Journey from Discouragement to Destiny

Key Verses
Judges 6:1–13

Lesson Overview
Israel was once again in bondage for their disobedience. God sent a prophet to call Israel to repentance, but they also needed a deliverer. God chose Gideon, an unlikely candidate in men's eyes, to deliver Israel from the Midianites. Gideon gathered Israel's army, and God thinned out the troops until the victory could only be a miracle of God. God used an unlikely general, and He received all the glory from the victory.

Lesson Aim
Many of us doubt our abilities and hide behind our feelings of inadequacy. We feel that God has a destiny for us to fulfill, but through our human reasoning, we do not see how we can reach that goal. That's what your journey for the faith is about. God knows what He has called you to do, and He knows exactly what qualities you need to fulfill that purpose. He promises to supply your every need and to strengthen your confidence in Him on your journey for the faith.

Lesson Goals
At the conclusion of this lesson, students should:
- Understand the hindrances of living in fear.
- Trust God with feelings of inadequacy or insecurity.

- Choose to allow God to grow and prove their faith.
- Recognize God's provision when they respond to him in faithful obedience.

Teaching Outline

I. The Paralysis of Fear
   A. Fear leads to isolation.
   B. Fear leads to discouragement.

II. The Proving of Faith
   A. Faith is not self-confident.
      1. The fearful were released.
      2. The negligent were released.
   B. Faith is God-confident.
      1. God saw Gideon's potential.
      2. God blessed Gideon's faith.

III. The Provision for the Faithful
   A. God provides wisdom.
      1. Stand in your place.
      2. Hold your trumpet and your light.
   B. God provides tenacity.

LESSON SEVEN

The Journey from Discouragement to Destiny

Text

Judges 6:1–13

Introduction

Chippie the parakeet never saw it coming. One second he was peacefully perched in his cage. The next he was sucked in, washed up, and blown over. Chippie's problems began when his owner decided to clean Chippie's cage with a vacuum cleaner. She removed the attachment from the end of the hose and stuck it in the cage. The phone rang, and she turned to pick it up. She'd barely said "hello," when "sssopp!" Chippie got sucked in. The bird owner gasped, put down the phone, turned off the vacuum, and opened the bag. There was Chippie, still alive, but stunned.

Since the bird was covered with dust and soot, she grabbed him and raced to the bathroom, turned on the faucet, and held Chippie under the running water. Then, realizing that Chippie was soaked and shivering, she did what any compassionate bird owner would do...she reached for the hair dryer and blasted her pet with hot air.

Poor Chippie never knew what hit him.

A few days after the trauma, the reporter who'd initially written about the event contacted Chippie's owner to see how the bird was recovering. "Well," she replied, "Chippie doesn't sing much anymore—he just sits and stares." (From *In the Eye of the Storm* by Max Lucado)

How do we move past our discouragement to discover our destiny? Many people today choose to wallow in discouragement, rather than accept God's help and move forward.

Gideon lived during the period of the judges—a time when Israel lived wickedly in the sight of God. The judges were discerning men who governed and directed the Israelites for 339 years from the days of Moses and Joshua until the time of Saul.

Verse 6 of our text tells us that the children of Israel were living in constant fear and impoverishment. This condition was a consequence of disobedience to the Lord, as is stated in verse 10.

We see similar problems in our own society today as many people are discouraged about the state of sin and despair in our country. We have lost our moral compass. We have taken our freedom and gone wild.

Illustration

In 2002, the state of Louisiana was sued by the ACLU for teaching abstinence. The ACLU believes this teaching is forcing a religion upon the students. (ACLU.org, May 31, 2007)

A recent article in a magazine published by Kaiser Permanente stated that sexually transmitted diseases are not a moral issue. In other words, "Being immoral is not immoral."

In 1970, there were 200,000 people in prison. As of 2008 there were 1.5 million (or as many as live in our fourth largest city—Houston).

The list of problems and the sin prevalent in our world today could go on. As Christians, how do we move from discouragement to fulfilling our God-given purposes? We can learn from the life of a man named Gideon. God called Gideon to lead the children of Israel out of discouragement to find their destiny. Although he was not a man of unusual faith and boldness, he willingly followed God on his journey for the faith.

I. The Paralysis of Fear

JUDGES 6:22–23

22 *And when Gideon perceived that he was an angel of the* LORD, *Gideon said, Alas, O Lord GOD! for because I have seen an angel of the* LORD *face to face.*
23 *And the* LORD *said unto him, Peace be unto thee; fear not: thou shalt not die.*

The command to "fear not" is given dozens of times in God's Word, yet many still suffer from the paralysis of fear! Gideon was one of those people. The circumstances in which he lived caused him to hide in desperation rather than trust God.

Illustration

Researchers at Johns Hopkins University reported that thirty years ago, the greatest fears of grade school children were:

1. Animals
2. Being in a dark room
3. High places
4. Strangers
5. Loud noises

Today, kids are afraid of the following:

1. Divorce
2. Nuclear war
3. Cancer
4. Pollution
5. Being mugged

The opposite of fear is faith. God does not call us to a spirit of fear, but rather to a spirit of faith. Notice the contrast between the two:

Fear	Faith
Weakens	Strengthens
Imprisons	Liberates
Paralyzes	Empowers
Disheartens	Encourages
Sickens	Heals

A. *Fear leads to isolation.*

JUDGES 6:11

11 And there came an angel of the LORD, *and sat under an oak which was in Ophrah, that pertained unto Joash the Abiezrite: and his son Gideon threshed wheat by the winepress, to hide it from the Midianites.*

Lesson Seven—From Discouragement to Destiny

When we first see Gideon, he is threshing wheat in a winepress, hiding from the Midianites. He was isolated and alone.

> **TEACHING TIP**
>
> *The Midianites were nomads who dwelt in the east and southeast region of the Dead Sea. Their genealogy is traced through Abraham's concubine, Keturah.*

Illustration

The story is told of a man on vacation who returned to his cabin from a hike. He was badly scratched and bruised.

"What happened?" asked his wife.

"I met a snake on the trail," the man answered.

"Don't you remember?" the woman responded. "Yesterday, the ranger told us that none of the snakes up here are poisonous."

"They don't have to be poisonous if they can make you jump off a twenty-foot cliff!"

This is not the time for Christians to "jump off a cliff" and live in isolation and fear! This is the time for us to take the gospel of Christ to every creature. Do not let the news headlines or worldly culture drive you to isolation. Determine to punch holes in the darkness by spreading God's love to a world dying in sin.

B. *Fear leads to discouragement.*

JUDGES 6:13

13 And Gideon said unto him, Oh my Lord, if the LORD be with us, why then is all this befallen us? and where be all his miracles which our fathers told us of, saying,

Did not the LORD *bring us up from Egypt? but now the* LORD *hath forsaken us, and delivered us into the hands of the Midianites.*

Gideon was obviously discouraged by the oppression of the Midianites. When we allow fear to reign in our hearts, discouragement is sure to follow. David was also a man who experienced much discouragement. Notice his prayer:

PSALM 89:49

49 Lord, where are thy former lovingkindnesses, which thou swarest unto David in thy truth?

The Bible tells us that God has not given us the spirit of fear. Are you afraid to take on a task God has laid on your heart? You can be sure that your fear did not come from Him. Second Timothy 1:7 says, *"For God hath not given us the spirit of fear; but of power, and of love, and of a sound mind."* Decide today to give your fears to the Lord. Do not linger in isolation and discouragement. Claim His promises and move forward in faith!

II. The Proving of Faith

ROMANS 10:17

17 So then faith cometh by hearing, and hearing by the word of God.

Faith is listening to what God says in His Word and then acting on it. True faith always requires action, which we see evidenced in Gideon's life.

Lesson Seven—From Discouragement to Destiny

When God first called Gideon, he responded with doubt and reservation. He saw no qualifications in himself to be the deliverer of Israel.

JUDGES 6:14–15
14 And the LORD looked upon him, and said, Go in this thy might, and thou shalt save Israel from the hand of the Midianites: have not I sent thee?
15 And he said unto him, Oh my Lord, wherewith shall I save Israel? behold, my family is poor in Manasseh, and I am the least in my father's house.

Gideon questioned whether God had the right person. His faith was weak at this point; however, God promised that He would be with him to help him. God wanted to strengthen Gideon's faith and trust in Him.

JUDGES 6:16
16 And the LORD said unto him, Surely I will be with thee, and thou shalt smite the Midianites as one man.

A. Faith is not self-confident.

JUDGES 7:2–4
2 And the LORD said unto Gideon, The people that are with thee are too many for me to give the Midianites into their hands, lest Israel vaunt themselves against me, saying, Mine own hand hath saved me.
3 Now therefore go to, proclaim in the ears of the people, saying, Whosoever is fearful and afraid, let him return and depart early from mount Gilead. And there returned of the people twenty and two thousand; and there remained ten thousand.
4 And the LORD said unto Gideon, The people are yet too many; bring them down unto the water, and I will try

them for thee there: and it shall be, that of whom I say unto thee, This shall go with thee, the same shall go with thee; and of whomsoever I say unto thee, This shall not go with thee, the same shall not go.

Although the Israelite army mustered only 32,000—one-sixth of the Midianite host—the number was too great. The Lord wanted Gideon and his men to learn true dependence upon Him.

In verse 3, we notice that the fearful were released from duty. God told Gideon he had too many soldiers. He was to send home all those who did not want to fight. Twenty-two thousand left, leaving Gideon with only 10,000. God was developing the faith of Gideon and of Israel. Gideon started with 32,000 and lost 22,000 in the first test!

In verse 6, we notice that the negligent were also released from duty. There were still too many soldiers. After another test, 9,700 were sent away. God had prepared Gideon to fight the Midianites with just three hundred men.

By faith, Gideon trusted God's directions. He is later mentioned in the great hall of faith in Hebrews 11.

Hebrews 11:32–34

32 And what shall I more say? for the time would fail me to tell of Gedeon, and of Barak, and of Samson, and of Jephthae; of David also, and Samuel, and of the prophets:
33 Who through faith subdued kingdoms, wrought righteousness, obtained promises, stopped the mouths of lions,
34 Quenched the violence of fire, escaped the edge of the sword, out of weakness were made strong, waxed valiant in fight, turned to flight the armies of the aliens.

Lesson Seven—From Discouragement to Destiny

> **Illustration**

Fifty two of the fifty five signers of the Declaration of Independence were believers in Christ. At the same time they declared independence from England they were declaring their dependence on God. When we declare our independence from human help or earthly efforts, we must declare our dependence on God.

What is the task God has for you? Do not let your timid spirit be an excuse for disobedience. Decide to cast your dependence on God, just as Gideon, our founding fathers, and hundreds of Christians throughout history did. He will never fail you!

B. Faith is God-confident.

HEBREW 11:6

6 *But without faith it is impossible to please him: for he that cometh to God must believe that he is, and that he is a rewarder of them that diligently seek him.*

God saw Gideon's potential. In Judges 6:12, he is referred to as a mighty man of valor. That was probably not how Gideon would have referred to himself. But God saw what He could accomplish through a willing vessel. God sees our potential as well. He wants us to put our faith and confidence in Him so He can develop it.

JUDGES 7:8–9

8 *So the people took victuals in their hand, and their trumpets: and he sent all the rest of Israel every man unto his tent, and retained those three hundred men: and the host of Midian was beneath him in the valley.*
9 *And it came to pass the same night, that the LORD said unto him, Arise, get thee down unto the host; for I have delivered it into thine hand.*

When it was time to obey God, Gideon's confidence in Him did not waver. He obeyed completely, even when the commands seemed irrational and unreasonable to the human way of thinking. Gideon followed the revelation of God, trusting that He would take care of him. He answered God's call and took up the challenge, realizing that His strength would come from the Lord.

Not only did God see Gideon's potential, He blessed Gideon's faith. In chapter seven, Gideon and God's army were delivered from the hands of the Midianites. When we step out in faith, God will never let us down. He always blesses true faith in action.

ROMANS 8:31

31 What shall we then say to these things? If God be for us, who can be against us?

God takes every person on a different journey of faith. Each person is designed as a special creation to fulfill a specific purpose. He does not call every believer to the same task. Your task will probably be different than Gideon's, yet it will still require confidence in God and will result in abundant blessings as we respond to Him.

III. The Provision for the Faithful

A. *God provides wisdom.*

JUDGES 7:19–21

19 So Gideon, and the hundred men that were with him, came unto the outside of the camp in the beginning of the middle watch; and they had but newly set the watch: and they blew the trumpets, and brake the pitchers that were in their hands.

Lesson Seven—From Discouragement to Destiny

20 And the three companies blew the trumpets, and brake the pitchers, and held the lamps in their left hands, and the trumpets in their right hands to blow withal: and they cried, The sword of the LORD, and of Gideon.
21 And they stood every man in his place round about the camp: and all the host ran, and cried, and fled.

God instructed Gideon to give each of the three hundred men a trumpet, a pitcher, and a torch. God told Gideon to surround the Midianites, each man in place. When he gave the signal (at the beginning of the middle watch, which was after midnight), they were to blow their trumpets, break the pitchers, and shout, *"The sword of the Lord and of Gideon."* Gideon and his army followed God's command.

God provided the wisdom for them to stand in their place. We see this in verse 21. God desires faithfulness from each of us. The Bible says in Proverbs 27:8, *"As a bird that wandereth from her nest, so is a man that wandereth from his place."* Man is prone to wander, yet with God's wisdom we can make choices that will help us remain faithful. May we claim God's wisdom to stay in our place—whether it be as a teacher, nursery worker, parent, friend, or encourager. God has a specific role for each of us, and He desires that we stay where He has put us.

God also provided wisdom to hold their trumpets and their lights. The army must have felt strange holding trumpets and lights in battle. You may feel as though you look strange in our world today.

Quote

Justice Antonin Scalia said, "Christians who actually live according to the Bible in the USA can expect to be viewed as fools."

Christianity and morals are despised in the society in which we live. Yet, God can give us wisdom to live righteously in a wicked world.

Quote

George Washington said, "It is impossible to righteously govern the world without God and the Bible."

The same is true in our individual lives. We need God and His Word to give us the wisdom needed to govern and guide our daily steps.

From a human perspective, God's battle plan for Gideon was not the method to use in conquering the Midianites. We most likely would have strategized and pursued full force with great weapons of war. Those who will gain confidence in God, however, must realize that God's wisdom is infinitely greater than our own. Notice the following verses:

Isaiah 55:8–9

8 For my thoughts are not your thoughts, neither are your ways my ways, saith the Lord.
9 For as the heavens are higher than the earth, so are my ways higher than your ways, and my thoughts than your thoughts.

We can thank the Lord that He will provide the wisdom we need in every situation in life. We simply must ask, and He will give liberally.

James 1:5

5 If any of you lack wisdom, let him ask of God, that giveth to all men liberally, and upbraideth not; and it shall be given him.

B. God provides tenacity.

JUDGES 8:1–4

1 And the men of Ephraim said unto him, Why hast thou served us thus, that thou calledst us not, when thou wentest to fight with the Midianites? And they did chide with him sharply.

2 And he said unto them, What have I done now in comparison of you? Is not the gleaning of the grapes of Ephraim better than the vintage of Abiezer?

3 God hath delivered into your hands the princes of Midian, Oreb and Zeeb: and what was I able to do in comparison of you? Then their anger was abated toward him, when he had said that.

4 And Gideon came to Jordan, and passed over, he, and the three hundred men that were with him, faint, yet pursuing them.

God provided the tenacity Gideon needed when he was criticized. If you do something for God, you will be criticized! Someone once said, "To avoid criticism, say nothing, do nothing, believe nothing."

2 TIMOTHY 3:12

12 Yea, and all that will live godly in Christ Jesus shall suffer persecution.

The Bible says in verse 4 that Gideon and his men were faint, yet they still pursued.

Man did not provide the help Gideon needed. We see in Judges 8:5–7 that the men of Succoth wouldn't help. In verse 9, the Bible records that the men of Penuel wouldn't help him either. God was the only help Gideon had or needed.

> **Illustration**
>
> A man came to D.L. Moody once and criticized him for the method he used in winning souls. Moody listened politely and then asked, "How would you do it?" The man, taken back by the question, quietly mumbled that he didn't do it. "Well," said Moody, "I prefer the way I do it to the way you don't do it."

2 CORINTHIANS 4:16–18

16 For which cause we faint not; but though our outward man perish, yet the inward man is renewed day by day.
17 For our light affliction, which is but for a moment, worketh for us a far more exceeding and eternal weight of glory;
18 While we look not at the things which are seen, but at the things which are not seen: for the things which are seen are temporal; but the things which are not seen are eternal.

Conclusion

God called Gladys to the mission field. She knew He wanted her to go to China to tell them about God's love. She attended the mission training school pending acceptance as a candidate, but she failed missionary training school. They told her that she was not qualified and refused to accept her as a missionary. Were they telling her God did not equip her to fulfill His purpose for her life? She refused to accept their decision and decided to trust God. Gladys was sure of her call and sure of her God. Taking a job as a maid, she saved money to buy a ticket to China. One day, she heard of an elderly missionary in China who was looking for someone to help her with her work.

Lesson Seven—From Discouragement to Destiny

Gladys left for China in 1932, during a time when Japan was at war with Russian and China. When Gladys finally arrived, the retired missionary was surprised to see her but put her to work immediately. She learned the Chinese language, a feat the mission board had said was impossible. Sharing the Gospel in surrounding villages, she began to take in unwanted children. The number of children under her care grew to one hundred. Through the circumstances of war, Gladys and the children had to flee to the safety of Siam over one hundred miles away. Gladys once again depended on God, and He showed Himself strong.

At the end of a life of reliance on God through many extreme circumstances, she wrote of herself, "My heart is full of praise that one so insignificant, uneducated, and ordinary in every way could be used to His glory for the blessing of His people in poor, persecuted China."

Like Gideon and his men, will you stand in your place? Will you pursue with purpose?

We do not have to be strong or mighty men of courage before God can use us. He does not look at our abilities and talents; He looks at our trust and obedience. By faith, we truly can move from discouragement to destiny.

Study Questions

1. According to Judges 6:12, how did God see Gideon?
   God saw Gideon as a mighty man of valor.

2. According to Judges 6:14–15, what were Gideon's objections to God's call?
   His family was poor and Gideon was weak, the least in his father's house.

3. What kind of effect does fear have on the life of a Christian?
   Fear paralyzes the Christian, making him ineffective in the Lord's work.

4. Fear led to two specific results in Gideon's life. What were they?
   Gideon's fear led to isolation and discouragement.

5. God proved Gideon's faith by removing human instruments and military strength. In your life, are you depending on something other than the Lord? If so, what is it and what steps can you take to become more "God-confident"?
   Answers will vary.

Lesson Seven—From Discouragement to Destiny

6. God promises His provision when we walk by faith. What two types of provision did God give to Gideon? *God provided Gideon with wisdom and tenacity.*

Memory Verse

2 TIMOTHY 1:7

7 For God hath not given us the spirit of fear; but of power, and of love, and of a sound mind.

LESSON EIGHT

The Journey to Jericho

Key Verses
Joshua 2:1–9

Lesson Overview
As Joshua and the children of Israel were claiming the land God had promised them, they came to a walled city called Jericho. This city had to be conquered if they were to possess the land. Before attacking, Joshua sent two spies into Jericho. The spies were soon within the city, mingling with the people and gathering information. The spies were found out and the city was on alert. When they turned into the home of a woman named Rahab, she hid them. Sending the soldiers on a futile search through the streets of the city, she went up to the roof and talked with the spies. She declared her belief that Israel's God was the one true God. Rahab asked for safety when they attacked the city. The spies made a pact with her that they would not destroy her family when they conquered Jericho.

Lesson Aim
Students should understand the change that salvation brings to the life of the believer. As new creatures in Christ, we must seek to live a life of faith demonstrated by our works.

Lesson Goals

At the conclusion of this lesson, students should:
- Understand man's sinful state before salvation.
- Remove any idols that would hinder spiritual growth.
- Appreciate God's work of redemption in saving sinners.
- Demonstrate true faith by godly actions.

Teaching Outline

I. The Reputation of Rahab
    A. A reputation of iniquity
    B. A reputation of idolatry

II. The Redemption of Rahab
    A. Her realization
    B. Her repentance

III. The Faith of Rahab
    A. To spare the spies
    B. To save her family

LESSON EIGHT

The Journey to Jericho

Text

Joshua 2:1–9

Introduction

Most people esteem diamonds for two attributes—hardness and brilliance. Diamonds have long been known for their indestructibility, but it was not until fairly recently that their brilliance was discovered. Diamonds are made of carbon, one of the most common elements on earth. Carbon is a solid, non-metallic element found in all living things. Carbon makes up roughly 18% of your body weight. Graphite (used in pencil lead) is a soft black mineral also made up of pure carbon. Why do we not place great value on pencil lead? What makes the two forms of carbon different?

Diamonds form about one hundred miles below the surface of the earth where there is just the right amount of pressure and heat. Carbon must be placed under at least 435,113 pounds per square inch of pressure at a temperature of at least 752° F. If these two conditions are not met, graphite instead of diamonds will result. The heat and pressure transform the carbon into a diamond.

When a person trusts Jesus as Saviour, he begins his journey for the faith. God takes the life of that believer and through the pressure of testing and the heat of trials, transforms a sinner into a mature child of God. In our lesson today, God takes the life of Rahab and changes her into a diamond that will let the brilliance of God's light shine through her life.

God had promised the land of Canaan to the children of Israel. There were many cities and peoples already occupying the land. Joshua, as their leader, was to lead them in conquering each city. God promised to be with Joshua. *"There shall not any man be able to stand before thee all the days of thy life: as I was with Moses, so I will be with thee: I will not fail thee, nor forsake thee"* (Joshua 1:5).

As Joshua led the people to the shores of the Jordan River, they were now just a few miles west of the formidable city of Jericho, surrounded and protected by a wall.

> **TEACHING TIP**
>
> *When Jericho was excavated in the late 1800s, archaeologists found remains of walls 30 feet high and 10–12 feet wide.*

As the children of Israel looked at this city, they must have wondered how they would conquer the enemy.

Lesson Eight—The Journey to Jericho

Illustration

"Oh, I sure am happy to see you," the little boy said to his grandmother at his mother's side. "Now maybe daddy will do the trick he has been promising us." The grandmother was curious. "What trick is that?" she asked. "I heard him tell mommy that he would climb the walls if you came to visit," the little boy answered.

Joshua and the army of Israel would not be able to simply climb the walls of Jericho. God's power was required for victory.

In our lesson today, we will not only see how the city fell, we will also learn how God touched the heart of one of the inhabitants of this pagan land. God loved each person in this giant and bustling city, including Rahab.

I. The Reputation of Rahab

When Joshua approached Jericho, he sent two spies to inspect the city. While there, they stayed at the house of Rahab.

A. A reputation of iniquity

It doesn't take long to discover the reputation of Rahab. It is quickly stated in this chapter.

Joshua 2:1

1 And Joshua the son of Nun sent out of Shittim two men to spy secretly, saying, Go view the land, even Jericho. And they went, and came into an harlot's house, named Rahab, and lodged there.

Rahab was a harlot, and she was known for her wicked lifestyle. She was a woman with a sin-filled life, yet God's mercy reached down to her, as we will see as our story unfolds.

Psalm 90:8
8 Thou hast set **our iniquities** before thee, our secret sins in the light of thy countenance.

Isaiah 59:2–4
2 But **your iniquities** have separated between you and your God, and your sins have hid his face from you, that he will not hear.
3 For your hands are defiled with blood, and your fingers with iniquity; your lips have spoken lies, your tongue hath muttered perverseness.
4 None calleth for justice, nor any pleadeth for truth: they trust in vanity, and speak lies; they conceive mischief, and **bring forth iniquity**.

The Lord knows the ways of man. The Bible declares that our sins are not hid from him. He sees even the secret sins. He knew the ways of Rahab, and He knows our ways as well.

B. A reputation of idolatry

Rahab also had a reputation of worshipping idols. Idolatry was a common practice among the nations of the world at that time. The Canaanites were idolatrous people, and Jericho was a land of idolatry. The people were condemned by God as idol worshippers.

Numbers 33:51–53
51 …When ye are passed over Jordan into the land of Canaan;

Lesson Eight—The Journey to Jericho

52 Then ye shall drive out all the inhabitants of the land from before you, and destroy all their pictures, and destroy all their molten images, and quite pluck down all their high places:
53 And ye shall dispossess the inhabitants of the land, and dwell therein: for I have given you the land to possess it.

An idol is defined as any image or figure consecrated as an object of worship. Idols were typically images made of wood, stone, or precious metal. In this land, there were wicked, sensual, and abominable pictures and molten images. God wanted the children of Israel to get rid of any image of idolatry when they possessed this land of Jericho.

> **Idol** (noun)
> any image or figure consecrated as an object of worship
>
> **worship** (verb)
> to ascribe worth

In this land in which we live, there is much idolatry today. Americans have their pictures and their idols as well. We are not far removed from the sin of Rahab's day. Just as God wanted the idols to be removed from Jericho, He wants the idols to be removed from our lives.

We may read of the Canaanites and of Rahab and condemn their idolatrous hearts. Yet, we all have something that can become an idol in our lives. Everyone has something that can potentially keep them from faith.

Idols of the heart can appear in many forms. Consider the following list:

Selfishness
Recreation and sports
A material possession
Education
A Relationship

Exodus 20:3

3 Thou shalt have no other gods before me.

> **Quote**
>
> *Today's idols are more in self than on the shelf.*

Rahab was a woman of iniquity living in a land of idolatry. We, like Rahab, would also have a poor reputation if it weren't for the grace of God saving us! Notice the wonderful redemption of Rahab.

II. The Redemption of Rahab

It doesn't matter where you've been or what you've done. God loves you! God will save anyone who will turn to Him.

A. Her realization

We read of Rahab's realization in Joshua 2:9.

Joshua 2:9

9 And she said unto the men, I know that the LORD hath given you the land, and that your terror is fallen upon us, and that all the inhabitants of the land faint because of you.

God had been working on Rahab's heart and had been revealing His power to her. We see evidence of this in her statement, "*I know that the LORD hath given you the land.*" The word *know* means to acknowledge or recognize.

God is constantly revealing Himself to this lost and dying world. In Rahab's time, He revealed Himself through drying up the Red Sea and through conquering the Egyptians. Acts such as these told the world that He was and is God.

God testifies in many ways and in all lands. He speaks through creation, declaring His existence. He testifies through his revealed Word. Every person has the ability to see God.

Let's examine the extent of Rahab's realization. First, she realized who the God of the Israelites was. She called Him "Lord." This is the name of God that is always associated with His salvation and deliverance.

No one will ever be saved until he recognizes his iniquity and until he knows that God has power to save. This is why soulwinners and teachers of God's Word must be thorough in their presentation of salvation.

Second, Rahab realized that Israel's God had given Israel the land. This reveals that Rahab saw Israel's God as a source of goodness, blessing, and power.

Rahab may have been a woman of great iniquity; nevertheless, she came to an understanding and acceptance of the truth. Just as Rahab, each of us must have a coming to the truth.

1 Timothy 2:4–5

4 *Who will have all men to be saved, and to come unto the knowledge of the truth.*

5 *For there is one God, and one mediator between God and men, the man Christ Jesus;*

Ephesians 4:17–18

17 *This I say therefore, and testify in the Lord, that ye henceforth walk not as other Gentiles walk, in the vanity of their mind,*

18 Having the understanding darkened, being alienated from the life of God through the ignorance that is in them, because of the blindness of their heart:

The conversion of Saul gives a wonderful example of one who came to the knowledge of truth. He had lived a life of cruel wickedness, yet when he realized and acknowledged who God was, his life changed.

ACTS 9:4–6
4 And he fell to the earth, and heard a voice saying unto him, Saul, Saul, why persecutest thou me?
5 And he said, Who art thou, Lord? And the Lord said, I am Jesus whom thou persecutest: it is hard for thee to kick against the pricks.
6 And he trembling and astonished said, Lord, what wilt thou have me to do? And the Lord said unto him, Arise, and go into the city, and it shall be told thee what thou must do.

B. *Her repentance*

Once Rahab acknowledged God, she repented of her sins.

JOSHUA 2:11
11 And as soon as we had heard these things, our hearts did melt, neither did there remain any more courage in any man, because of you: for the LORD your God, he is God in heaven above, and in earth beneath.

When the people in Jericho heard about the children of Israel and the miracles God had performed on their behalf, Rahab said *"our hearts did melt."*

All of Jericho saw God's mighty works, but only one believed. This is significant because only Rahab responded in repentance. She turned from her old life and placed her faith in the God of the Israelites. She saw, as did all the citizens of Jericho, the coming battle. All of Jericho had heard about Israel's God, yet even their fear did not motivate them to repent, except for Rahab.

Quote

"If God's today be too soon for thy repentance, thy tomorrow may be too late for God's acceptance."—D.L. Moody

1 THESSALONIANS 1:9
9   For they themselves shew of us what manner of entering in we had unto you, and how ye turned to God from idols to serve the living and true God;

When a person is saved, he is turning to God in faith while simultaneously turning from idols. When Rahab turned to God, she turned her back on the idols of Canaan.

2 CORINTHIANS 5:17
17   Therefore if any man be in Christ, he is a new creature: old things are passed away; behold, all things are become new.

The world today needs dedicated Christians who will rid themselves of idols and their old ways of living. When Rahab left Jericho, she didn't ask to take her idols with her. She left clean from her former ways. May we do the same!

Quote

"There is no growth without challenge, and there is no challenge without change."—Warren Wiersbe

> **Illustration**
>
> The story is told of a young girl who accepted Christ as her Saviour and applied for membership in a local church. "Were you a sinner before you received the Lord Jesus into your life?" inquired an old deacon.
>
> "Yes, sir," she replied.
>
> "Well, are you still a sinner?"
>
> "To tell you the truth, I feel I'm a greater sinner than ever."
>
> "Then what real change have you experienced?"
>
> "I don't quite know how to explain it," she said, "except I used to be a sinner running after sin, but now that I am saved, I'm a sinner running from sin!" She was received into the fellowship of the church, and she proved by her consistent life that she was truly converted.

HEBREWS 11:31

31 By faith the harlot Rahab perished not with them that believed not, when she had received the spies with peace.

Rahab was saved—redeemed—because of her faith in God. She saw her condition, and then placed her faith in the right person—the God of Israel. (The object of faith is more important than our faith!)

III. The Faith of Rahab

When faith in Christ is present, He changes our reputation! Rahab had a working faith. Her faith was evidenced in her actions.

JAMES 2:17

17 Even so faith, if it hath not works, is dead, being alone.

Her works did not save her. Nevertheless, her salvation was demonstrated by her works. It was evidence to all that she trusted God. Is there evidence of salvation in your life?

A. *To spare the spies*

JOSHUA 2:12–15

12 Now therefore, I pray you, swear unto me by the LORD, since I have shewed you kindness, that ye will also shew kindness unto my father's house, and give me a true token:

13 And that ye will save alive my father, and my mother, and my brethren, and my sisters, and all that they have, and deliver our lives from death.

14 And the men answered her, Our life for yours, if ye utter not this our business. And it shall be, when the LORD hath given us the land, that we will deal kindly and truly with thee.

15 Then she let them down by a cord through the window: for her house was upon the town wall, and she dwelt upon the wall.

Rahab demonstrated faith to spare the spies of Israel. She trusted the word of the spies and hung the scarlet rope out her window. She risked her life for the sake of hiding the spies. This was an act of faith demonstrated by her works.

JAMES 2:25

25 Likewise also was not Rahab the harlot justified by works, when she had received the messengers, and had sent them out another way?

> **Quote**
>
> *"Faith shows itself in 'the whole personality'... True saving faith involves 'the whole personality': the mind is instructed, the emotions are stirred, and the will then acts in obedience to God."*—Martin Lloyd Jones

B. To save her family

JOSHUA 2:12–13

12 Now therefore, I pray you, swear unto me by the LORD, since I have shewed you kindness, that ye will also shew kindness unto my father's house, and give me a true token:

13 And that ye will save alive my father, and my mother, and my brethren, and my sisters, and all that they have, and deliver our lives from death.

JOSHUA 2:17–18

17 And the men said unto her, We will be blameless of this thine oath which thou hast made us swear.

18 Behold, when we come into the land, thou shalt bind this line of scarlet thread in the window which thou didst let us down by: and thou shalt bring thy father, and thy mother, and thy brethren, and all thy father's household, home unto thee.

Rahab also had faith to save her family. She heard the word of the spies. She knew what would happen to her city, and she acted in faith. She boldly asked the spies to spare her family from the destruction that was imminent.

> **Quote**
>
> *"Faith does not operate in the realm of the possible. There is no glory for God in that which is humanly possible. Faith begins where man's power ends."*—George Muller

Lesson Eight—The Journey to Jericho

Joshua 6:22–23

22 But Joshua had said unto the two men that had spied out the country, Go into the harlot's house, and bring out thence the woman, and all that she hath, as ye sware unto her.
23 And the young men that were spies went in, and brought out Rahab, and her father, and her mother, and her brethren, and all that she had; and they brought out all her kindred, and left them without the camp of Israel.

Joshua 6:25

25 And Joshua saved Rahab the harlot alive, and her father's household, and all that she had; and she dwelleth in Israel even unto this day; because she hid the messengers, which Joshua sent to spy out Jericho.

Rahab's act of putting the scarlet rope outside her window is a reminder of the blood atonement.

Exodus 12:13

13 And the blood shall be to you for a token upon the houses where ye are: and when I see the blood, I will pass over you, and the plague shall not be upon you to destroy you, when I smite the land of Egypt.

Hebrews 9:22

22 And almost all things are by the law purged with blood; and without shedding of blood is no remission.

Ephesians 1:7

7 In whom we have redemption through his blood, the forgiveness of sins, according to the riches of his grace;

Conclusion

A few days after Rahab's encounter with the spies, Jericho was completely destroyed, but Rahab had been saved by faith.

Notice two other outcomes in Rahab's life:

1. God placed her in the hall of faith.

   JOSHUA 2:12
   12 Now therefore, I pray you, swear unto me by the LORD, since I have shewed you kindness, that ye will also shew kindness unto my father's house, and give me a true token:

   Rahab's security was based upon her faith in the God of Israel, and her token of that faith was the scarlet cord hanging out her window.

   HEBREWS 11:31
   31 By faith the harlot Rahab perished not with them that believed not, when she had received the spies with peace.

2. She married an Israelite and was included in the Messianic line of Christ.

   MATTHEW 1:5–6
   5 And Salmon begat Booz of Rachab; and Booz begat Obed of Ruth; and Obed begat Jesse;
   6 And Jesse begat David the king; and David the king begat Solomon of her that had been the wife of Urias;

These two acts are glorious pictures of the wonderful grace of God! May we remember these truths as we seek to live out our faith on a daily basis!

LESSON EIGHT—THE JOURNEY TO JERICHO

Study Questions

1. Describe Rahab's reputation before she was saved.
   Rahab was a harlot who lived in iniquity and who practiced idolatry.

2. An idol is anyone or anything that takes the place of God in your heart. Take a moment to search your heart and identify anything that may be an idol in your life. Write out a prayer to God, surrendering that idol to Him.
   Answers will vary.

3. According to Joshua 2:9, what did Rahab realize or acknowledge?
   Rahab acknowledged who God is and also realized that God had given Israel the land of Jericho.

4. How did Rahab demonstrate her repentance?
   Rahab turned from her idols to serve the living and true God.

5. Write out 1 Thessalonians 1:9 in the space provided.
   1 THESSALONIANS 1:9
   9 For they themselves shew of us what manner of entering in we had unto you, and how ye turned to God from idols to serve the living and true God;

6. If our faith lacks works, how does the Bible describe it in James 2:17?
   The Bible says if our faith does not have works it is dead.

7. What two actions did Rahab perform that proved her faith in God?
Rahab had faith to hide the spies and to save her family from the destruction that would come on Jericho.

8. Read Hebrews 11:31 and Matthew 1:5–6. According to these passages, what two blessings did Rahab receive?
Rahab's name was recorded in the Hebrews 11 Hall of Faith, testifying of her belief in God, and she was included in the Messianic line of Christ.

Memory Verse

2 Corinthians 5:17

17 Therefore if any man be in Christ, he is a new creature: old things are passed away; behold, all things are become new.

LESSON NINE

The Journey to Shiloh

Key Verses

1 Samuel 3:1–13

Lesson Overview

After earnestly praying for many years, Hannah bore a son, Samuel, and kept her promise to God. She gave Samuel back to God to serve Him in Shiloh. Because of his obedience and dedication in serving, God called Samuel to be the priest of Israel. Throughout his life, Samuel continued to obey and serve God. He faithfully declared righteousness and showed people the way of God.

Lesson Aim

To some, serving God has become something that is added to regular duties. For the Christian, serving God should be the umbrella under which every task is performed. Whether we are dictating a letter, balancing the books, nursing a patient, or changing a diaper, all is to be done as a service to God.

Lesson Goals

At the conclusion of this lesson, students should:
- Realize that a journey of obedience begins with surrender and dedication.

- Strive to be in a position to hear God's commands and direction.
- Understand the holiness of God and seek to cleanse themselves from any unconfessed sin.
- Determine to do God's work God's way, using His established order and methods.
- Seek to be a shining light for God in a world darkened by sin.

Teaching Outline

I. The Calling of Samuel
   A. The hearing of Samuel
      1. He was assisted by Eli.
      2. He was approached by God.
   B. The holiness of God
      1. God's pronouncement against Eli
      2. God's purpose for Samuel

II. The Cleansing of the People
   A. A conditional covenant
   B. A call for help

III. The Concern of Samuel
   A. The people refused the hand of the Lord.
   B. Saul replaced the order of the Lord.

LESSON NINE

The Journey to Shiloh

Text

1 Samuel 3:1–13

Introduction

We first learn about Samuel in one of the great stories of the Bible: the story of Hannah and her prayer for a son.

Hannah was a woman who was barren. She had not been able to bear a son for Elkanah. Although Elkanah loved her more than he loved his second wife Peninnah, Hannah was constantly distressed because of her inability to have a child. She went to the tabernacle and there wept and begged God for a son. As Hannah poured out her heart to God, she vowed that if He would hear and give her a son, she would give him back to God to serve in the tabernacle.

1 Samuel 1:11

11 *And she vowed a vow, and said, O Lord of hosts, if thou wilt indeed look on the affliction of thine handmaid, and remember me, and not forget thine handmaid, but wilt give unto thine handmaid a man child, then I will give him unto the Lord all the days of his life, and there shall no razor come upon his head.*

When God gave Hannah a son, she kept her promise. She gave Samuel back to the Lord to serve Him in the tabernacle. Hannah displayed a true act of surrender in giving Samuel to the Lord. Throughout his life, Samuel demonstrated great surrender by serving God in Israel. We, too, should be willing to surrender all to God. Every member of our body is to be surrendered to God's control and used to serve Him.

Our tongue should sing God's praise and should speak honest, kind words that will edify others.

Psalm 34:13

13 *Keep thy tongue from evil, and thy lips from speaking guile.*

Our hands should be busily employed in service to others.

Ecclesiastes 9:10

10 *Whatsoever thy hand findeth to do, do it with thy might…*

Our feet should not run to places of iniquity but should be ready to walk in the paths of righteousness.

Ephesians 4:17

17 *This I say therefore, and testify in the Lord, that ye henceforth walk not as other Gentiles walk, in the vanity of their mind,*

Our eyes should survey God's glory in creation rather than the depravity of the world.

Lesson Nine—The Journey to Shiloh

Psalm 19:1
1 *The heavens declare the glory of God; and the firmament sheweth his handywork.*

Our ears should listen for the voice of God as He speaks through His Word and preaching.

John 10:27
27 *My sheep hear my voice, and I know them, and they follow me:*

Let God have every part of you—your heart and your dearest possessions!

Romans 12:1–2
1 *I beseech you therefore, brethren, by the mercies of God, that ye present your bodies a living sacrifice, holy, acceptable unto God, which is your reasonable service.*
2 *And be not conformed to this world: but be ye transformed by the renewing of your mind, that ye may prove what is that good, and acceptable, and perfect, will of God.*

Samuel grew and was greatly used of God throughout his life. During the period of the Judges, the tabernacle was at Shiloh. There, God raised up a man who would stand for Him amidst the religious and political corruption of his day. During a time when the people of God strayed, Samuel stood.

I. The Calling of Samuel

After God provided a son for Hannah and her husband, Hannah gave Samuel to the Lord. From an early age, Samuel grew up in the tabernacle in Shiloh.

1 Samuel 3:1–4

1 And the child Samuel ministered unto the Lord before Eli. And the word of the Lord was precious in those days; there was no open vision.

2 And it came to pass at that time, when Eli was laid down in his place, and his eyes began to wax dim, that he could not see;

3 And ere the lamp of God went out in the temple of the Lord, where the ark of God was, and Samuel was laid down to sleep;

4 That the Lord called Samuel: and he answered, Here am I.

A. *The hearing of Samuel*

While Samuel was lying down to sleep, he heard the voice of the Lord calling out to him. Thinking it was Eli, Samuel ran to him. In verses 5–9, we see that he was assisted by Eli.

1 Samuel 3:5–9

5 And he ran unto Eli, and said, Here am I; for thou calledst me. And he said, I called not; lie down again. And he went and lay down.

6 And the Lord called yet again, Samuel. And Samuel arose and went to Eli, and said, Here am I; for thou didst call me. And he answered, I called not, my son; lie down again.

7 Now Samuel did not yet know the Lord, neither was the word of the Lord yet revealed unto him.

8 And the Lord called Samuel again the third time. And he arose and went to Eli, and said, Here am I; for thou didst call me. And Eli perceived that the Lord had called the child.

9 Therefore Eli said unto Samuel, Go, lie down: and it shall be, if he call thee, that thou shalt say, Speak, Lord; for thy servant heareth. So Samuel went and lay down in his place.

Lesson Nine—The Journey to Shiloh

Up to this point in Samuel's life, he did not know the Lord, nor had the Lord revealed His Word to him. This is why Samuel did not discern between the Lord talking to him and Eli calling for him.

First Samuel 3:10 gives record of Samuel as he was approached by God.

1 SAMUEL 3:10
10 And the LORD came, and stood, and called as at other times, Samuel, Samuel. Then Samuel answered, Speak; for thy servant heareth.

The Lord *"stood"*—He stationed Himself where Samuel could not only hear but could also see who was talking. The Lord called out to Samuel as before, saying, "Samuel, Samuel."

Illustration

There was a man who was caught in a flash flood and was stranded on the top of his house. He prayed and asked the Lord to get him to safety. Just then a man in a boat came by and offered to free him from his roof. The man said, "No I am waiting for the Lord." A little while later a helicopter came by and again the man refused to be rescued. Pretty soon the waters overcame him and he drowned.

When he got to Heaven, he said to the Lord, "I asked you to rescue me and you didn't come for me." The Lord said, "I sent a boat and helicopter for you."

People often ask, "Why doesn't God speak to me?" God is more than willing to speak to us today through His Word and His Spirit, but we often become so occupied that we do not hear when God is trying to get our attention. May we seek to be in a position to hear the voice of the Lord when He speaks to us.

B. The holiness of God

Quote

"A holy life will make the deepest impression. Lighthouses blow no horns, they just shine."—D.L. Moody

Eli was the same high priest who had blessed Elkanah and Hannah when she prayed for a son. He served God many years but allowed his sons to bring wickedness into the house of the Lord. He was aware of their sin but did not stop it. The iniquity of Eli's sons intensified daily. Eli chose to ignore their sin, allowing them to display it in the tabernacle, and God condemned him for this. He made a pronouncement against Eli to Samuel.

1 SAMUEL 3:12–14

12 In that day I will perform against Eli all things which I have spoken concerning his house: when I begin, I will also make an end.

13 For I have told him that I will judge his house for ever for the iniquity which he knoweth; because his sons made themselves vile, and he restrained them not.

14 And therefore I have sworn unto the house of Eli, that the iniquity of Eli's house shall not be purged with sacrifice nor offering for ever.

Not only did God make a proclamation against Eli, He also stated His purpose for Samuel. Samuel had been faithful; therefore, God called on him to serve. His life had been clean, making him a vessel fit to be used of the Lord.

Lesson Nine—The Journey to Shiloh

2 Timothy 2:20–21
20 But in a great house there are not only vessels of gold and of silver, but also of wood and of earth; and some to honour, and some to dishonour.
21 If a man therefore purge himself from these, he shall be a vessel unto honour, sanctified, and meet for the master's use, and prepared unto every good work.

Samuel was given to God when he was a child. His parents dedicated him to serve God all the days of his life. He accepted this commitment and led a pure life, a life that was free from sin and worldliness. He kept his heart, mind, and body pure. He was a clean vessel available to be used by God at any time.

Samuel was a ready listener to God's Word. In stark contrast to Eli's sons, who were disobedient and disrespectful, Samuel had a reverence for the things of God.

1 Samuel 2:22, 26
22 Now Eli was very old, and heard all that his sons did unto all Israel; and how they lay with the women that assembled at the door of the tabernacle of the congregation.
26 And the child Samuel grew on, and was in favour both with the Lord, and also with men.

As Samuel served in the tabernacle, he undoubtedly had many jobs. One of which was to minister to Eli. The priest was getting older and needed help and attention. Eli's own sons had not been restrained from their sin causing their wickedness to pollute the tabernacle worship. Samuel, however, was faithful in serving and was not infected by the wicked behavior of Eli's sons. His purity and willing service to God is a sharp contrast to the wickedness and selfish perversion of Eli's sons.

God's second purpose for Samuel was to speak. We see this purpose revealed in 1 Samuel 3:18–19:

1 Samuel 3:17–19
17 And he said, What is the thing that the Lord hath said unto thee? I pray thee hide it not from me: God do so to thee, and more also, if thou hide any thing from me of all the things that he said unto thee.
18 And Samuel told him every whit, and hid nothing from him. And he said, It is the Lord: let him do what seemeth him good.
19 And Samuel grew, and the Lord was with him, and did let none of his words fall to the ground.

The true test of a prophet of God in Israel was if he gave every word which the Lord revealed to him. As a prophet of God, Samuel did not let one word drop from all that God had told him. He boldly declared and spoke the Words of the Lord.

Deuteronomy 18:20–22
20 But the prophet, which shall presume to speak a word in my name, which I have not commanded him to speak, or that shall speak in the name of other gods, even that prophet shall die.
21 And if thou say in thine heart, How shall we know the word which the Lord hath not spoken?
22 When a prophet speaketh in the name of the Lord, if the thing follow not, nor come to pass, that is the thing which the Lord hath not spoken, but the prophet hath spoken it presumptuously: thou shalt not be afraid of him.

Samuel was God's representative to the children of Israel. He spoke the words of the Lord without leaving anything out. He stood for God when the people obeyed, and he stood for God when they refused to obey. Samuel proclaimed their unrighteousness without compromise. He was steadfast and unwavering in his obedience to God and in his declaration of God's promises.

1 Corinthians 15:58
58 Therefore, my beloved brethren, be ye stedfast, unmoveable, always abounding in the work of the Lord, forasmuch as ye know that your labour is not in vain in the Lord.

II. The Cleansing of the People

The cleansing of the people was one of Samuel's first great acts as a leader after the death of Eli.

A. *A conditional covenant*

1 Samuel 7:2–3
2 And it came to pass, while the ark abode in Kirjathjearim, that the time was long; for it was twenty years: and all the house of Israel lamented after the Lord.
3 And Samuel spake unto all the house of Israel, saying, If ye do return unto the Lord with all your hearts, then put away the strange gods and Ashtaroth from among you, and prepare your hearts unto the Lord, and serve him only: and he will deliver you out of the hand of the Philistines.

Samuel told the people of Israel that if they would cleanse themselves, God would heal their land. This covenant centered around the removal of Israel's sin of idolatry. They had been worshipping the pagan gods and goddesses, Ashtaroth being one of them.

This covenant was also formed because the Ark of the Covenant had been kept in Kirjath-jearim for twenty years, and *"all the house of Israel lamented after the Lord."* Israel wanted the Lord to deliver them from the Philistines (v. 3c).

Judge 13:1
1 And the children of Israel did evil again in the sight of the Lord; and the Lord delivered them into the hand of the Philistines forty years.

This covenant was conditional. Samuel gives the conditions:

- Israel must return to the Lord with all their hearts.
- They must put away the strange gods and Ashtaroth from among them.
- They must prepare their hearts unto the Lord and serve only Him.

Israel's mourning brought them to a point of confession and repentance for their sins.

B. A call for help

1 Samuel 7:8–10
8 And the children of Israel said to Samuel, Cease not to cry unto the Lord our God for us, that he will save us out of the hand of the Philistines.
9 And Samuel took a sucking lamb, and offered it for a burnt offering wholly unto the Lord: and Samuel cried unto the Lord for Israel; and the Lord heard him.
10 And as Samuel was offering up the burnt offering, the Philistines drew near to battle against Israel: but the Lord thundered with a great thunder on that day upon

the Philistines, and discomfited them; and they were smitten before Israel.

It is important to note that before Samuel intervened for the people, they had to put away their sins (v. 4). Before we ask God for help, we must confess our sins as well. We cannot expect God to work on our behalf when we have ignored Him and allowed sin to come into our lives.

PSALM 66:18
18 If I regard iniquity in my heart, the Lord will not hear me:

The Israelites understood that they needed God's help in conquering the enemy. At this time in history, the Philistines were the only people in Palestine who knew how to work with iron. They had iron chariots and weapons, which would make them powerful opponents against Israel. However, iron also conducts electricity quite well, and if God thundered (v. 10), thunder would be accompanied by lightning! God answered the call of His people that day and discomfited the Philistines.

Samuel recognized God's power, and he understood that the defeat of the Philistines was a direct result of God's help. So, he set up a memorial rock and named it Ebenezer which means "Stone of help."

1 SAMUEL 7:12
12 Then Samuel took a stone, and set it between Mizpeh and Shen, and called the name of it Ebenezer, saying, Hitherto hath the LORD helped us.

PSALM 18:2
2 The LORD is my rock, and my fortress, and my deliverer; my God, my strength, in whom I will trust; my buckler, and the horn of my salvation, and my high tower.

III. The Concern of Samuel

As time went on, the people of Israel demanded a king so they could be like the other nations. This demand was cause for great concern in the heart of Samuel.

1 Samuel 8:19–20

19 Nevertheless the people refused to obey the voice of Samuel; and they said, Nay; but we will have a king over us;
20 That we also may be like all the nations; and that our king may judge us, and go out before us, and fight our battles.

A. The people refused the hand of the Lord.

1 Samuel 12:8–9

8 When Jacob was come into Egypt, and your fathers cried unto the Lord, then the Lord sent Moses and Aaron, which brought forth your fathers out of Egypt, and made them dwell in this place.
9 And when they forgat the Lord their God, he sold them into the hand of Sisera, captain of the host of Hazor, and into the hand of the Philistines, and into the hand of the king of Moab, and they fought against them.

The children of Israel forgot God and the mighty acts He had performed on their behalf.

Samuel reminded the people that God was the one who sent their human leaders such as Moses and Aaron to lead them through the wilderness. He reminded the people that God was the source of their deliverance from their enemies.

Samuel also reminded Israel that when they were right with God, a judge was sent to help with their problems, and there was peace. But when Israel forgot the Lord, then God sent the nations around them to discomfort them until they repented and came back to the Lord.

Yet, the people refused the hand of the Lord in their lives.

1 Samuel 12:12

12 *And when ye saw that Nahash the king of the children of Ammon came against you, ye said unto me, Nay; but a king shall reign over us: when the Lord your God was your king.*

B. Saul replaced the order of the Lord.

1 Samuel 13:8–12

8 *And he tarried seven days, according to the set time that Samuel had appointed: but Samuel came not to Gilgal; and the people were scattered from him.*
9 *And Saul said, Bring hither a burnt offering to me, and peace offerings. And he offered the burnt offering.*
10 *And it came to pass, that as soon as he had made an end of offering the burnt offering, behold, Samuel came; and Saul went out to meet him, that he might salute him.*
11 *And Samuel said, What hast thou done? And Saul said, Because I saw that the people were scattered from me, and that thou camest not within the days appointed, and that the Philistines gathered themselves together at Michmash;*
12 *Therefore said I, The Philistines will come down now upon me to Gilgal, and I have not made supplication unto the Lord: I forced myself therefore, and offered a burnt offering.*

God gave Israel their request for a king, and Saul became the first earthly king of Israel.

In 1 Samuel 13, we see Saul a few years into his reign. He was at Michmash and had been waiting for Samuel for seven days. In a moment of crisis, when Samuel did not come, Saul took things into his own hands.

First, He lacked trust in God's instructions through Samuel and did not wait as he was instructed. (This had been his problem from the start! He did not obey.) Saul ignored the words of Samuel, and he trusted his senses rather than God's commands.

Then, he chose to usurp the priesthood by offering a sacrifice! Saul replaced the order of the Lord by taking Samuel's place and performing priestly duties. He took lightly the order by which God had established the sacrifices.

Illustration

Phillip Brooks, a famous pastor of the last century, was in his office, pacing the floor, frustrated. Somebody walked in and saw him and asked, "What's the matter, Pastor?" He said, "I'm in a hurry and God isn't!"

God has an order and method of doing His work. If this were not so, then it would not matter how a man got saved as long as he was sincere about it. Often, people try to replace God's way with their own way of salvation. They become religious but miss the truth. Cain wanted to offer the fruits of his labor, not what was required by the Lord. He did that which was right in his own eyes, just as many men do what they think is right in their own eyes.

ACTS 4:12

12 Neither is there salvation in any other: for there is none other name under heaven given among men, whereby we must be saved.

May we determine to learn from the mistake of Saul and choose to follow God's order and methods in every aspect of our lives.

Samuel rebuked Saul for replacing God's order.

1 Samuel 13:13–14

13 And Samuel said to Saul, Thou hast done foolishly: thou hast not kept the commandment of the Lord thy God, which he commanded thee: for now would the Lord have established thy kingdom upon Israel for ever.

14 But now thy kingdom shall not continue: the Lord hath sought him a man after his own heart, and the Lord hath commanded him to be captain over his people, because thou hast not kept that which the Lord commanded thee.

Proverbs 14:12

12 There is a way which seemeth right unto a man, but the end thereof are the ways of death.

Conclusion

The Statue of Liberty, given to the United States by France in 1876, serves as a symbol of freedom and liberty to immigrants entering New York Harbor. However, few people know that from November 22, 1886, until March 1, 1902, the Statue of Liberty was an operational lighthouse. Ships were guided by the silent, steady light of Lady Liberty's torch. The Statue of Liberty's torch stood 305 feet above sea level. Her nine electric arcs could be seen for twenty-four miles out to sea.

Lighthouses are often built in desolate, out-of-the way places. They serve their purpose with consistency and diligence. A lighthouse is designed to withstand the worst storms and still keep shining. The light shines quietly and constantly to pierce the darkness as a beacon of hope for weary sailors. It is brightest during the darkest storms.

Throughout our journeys of faith, God prepares us to be a lighthouse in a world darkened by wickedness and sin. Each trial and test brings us closer to God, making our light shine brighter for Him.

Samuel was an example of a holy light in Israel. His consistent purity exposed the wickedness and indifference of Israel and shone forth with a pure, clear light. Samuel spent His life showing God's ways to a people and a king who wanted their own way.

Samuel relinquished all of his perceived rights and desires to follow God's plan for his life. His journey for the faith models a journey that God calls every believer to experience.

Lesson Nine—The Journey to Shiloh

Study Questions

1. What characteristic is evident in the lives of both Hannah and Samuel?
   Surrender (or dedication) was a prominent characteristic in the lives of Hannah and Samuel.

2. God had two primary purposes for Samuel which he accomplished throughout his life. What were they?
   God's two purposes for Samuel were to stand and to speak.

3. One of God's purposes for Samuel was to speak His words, not letting one fall to the ground. Are you faithful to tell others of God's plan of salvation? What can you do this week to share His Gospel message with those around you?
   Answers will vary.

4. As seen in our lesson, what must we do before we call upon the Lord for help?
   Before we call upon God's help, we must confess our sin.

5. Write out Psalm 66:18 in the space provided below. If there is any iniquity in your heart, take a moment right now to confess it to the Lord.

   Psalm 66:18
   18 If I regard iniquity in my heart, the Lord will not hear me:

6. Briefly describe Saul's actions that replaced the order of the Lord.
Saul did not wait for Samuel as he was commanded, and he offered a burnt sacrifice in Samuel's stead.

7. Name an obvious example of the children of Israel refusing the hand of the Lord.
The children of Israel refused the hand of the Lord by demanding a king.

8. God called Samuel to a lifetime of service for Him. Has God called you to a particular area of service? Are you performing it out of a heart of love for Him? Take a moment and write a quick evaluation of your service to God in light of Samuel's sacrificial service in Shiloh and throughout his life.
Answers will vary.

Memory Verses

1 PETER 1:14–16

14 As obedient children, not fashioning yourselves according to the former lusts in your ignorance:
15 But as he which hath called you is holy, so be ye holy in all manner of conversation;
16 Because it is written, Be ye holy; for I am holy.

LESSON TEN

The Journey to the Valley of Elah

Key Verse

1 Samuel 16:1–13

Lesson Overview

David was a young lad who obeyed God completely. He was a man after God's own heart, and God chose him to be the next king of Israel. God took David on a journey that caused his confidence in Him to grow. His most well known battle was with Goliath, the giant Philistine in the Valley of Elah. Young David was the instrument God used to defeat the giant and give glory to God.

Lesson Aim

Battles in the Christian life are inevitable, but as we cultivate hearts for God, we are given a purpose. We are able to live for a holy cause. Along the course of our journeys, God will prepare us for these battles. Then, he will give us the power to prevail for His glory!

Lesson Goals

At the conclusion of this lesson, students should:
- Desire to have a heart for God.
- Determine to fulfill God's calling no matter the cost.

- Know their God-given cause and understand that some will challenge it.
- Accept times of preparation for greater battles and victories.
- Seek to honor God in the victories given along the journey.

Teaching Outline

I. David's Calling
  A. The purpose of David's calling
    1. Because Saul was the king chosen of the people
    2. Because God was looking for a man after His own heart
  B. The process of David's calling
    1. The selection of David
    2. The sanctification of David

II. David's Cause
  A. His cause was for the faith.
  B. His cause was challenged.
    1. David was criticized by his brother.
    2. David was challenged by Saul.

III. David's Conflict
  A. David's preparation for battle
    1. By previous battles
    2. With proven methods
  B. David's power in battle
    1. David's trust was in the Lord.
    2. David's desire was to glorify God.
  C. David's prevailing in battle

LESSON TEN

The Journey to the Valley of Elah

Text

1 Samuel 16:1–13

Introduction

The majesty of the giant redwood trees in Northern California can quiet even the noisiest sightseer. The mere size of these enormous trees is enough to strike awe in the heart. The tallest redwood in the world measured more than 378 feet in the year 2000. Some coastal redwoods have been growing for more than 2000 years.

What was happening 2000 years ago? Julius Caesar was ruler of the Roman Empire. Jesus was born in a manger. Some of the Redwood trees were around during the time of the first church. To think of all the history that occurred during the lifetime of a redwood!

When we ponder the immensity and tenacity of these trees, we can only be reminded of the power of God who created such a wonder. No known killing diseases infect the redwoods. Any insects associated with them cause insignificant damage. Fire is their worst enemy, but even fire cannot kill a giant redwood. The bark of the tree is too thick. Little can harm a redwood.

David was a man after God's own heart. No king in Israel's history was more loved, mentioned, or compared to than David. He became a giant for God among men. His heart was so focused on God that nothing could destroy his passion for Him. He stood firm when ridiculed for God's sake. He stood boldly against those who would defame His God. This man of God was used in a tremendous way to establish the faith of Israel and bring this nation out of obscurity and into a world power in the Near East. David was an example of Christian service we should all follow.

Last week, we learned that Israel, wanting to be like the other nations, had demanded a king. Samuel anointed Saul as Israel's king. A few years into his reign, Saul organized and commanded Israel's army to fight an important battle against the Philistines. A time was appointed for Samuel, the high priest, to offer a sacrifice asking for God's blessing and help in the battle. Samuel told Saul he would come in seven days to bless the army. Saul waited for seven long days while the vastly superior army of the Philistines prepared for battle. The trembling Israelites were hiding in caves, mountains, and pits.

1 Samuel 13:6–7

6 *When the men of Israel saw that they were in a strait, (for the people were distressed,) then the people did hide themselves in caves, and in thickets, and in rocks, and in high places, and in pits.*

7 *And some of the Hebrews went over Jordan to the land of Gad and Gilead. As for Saul, he was yet in Gilgal, and all the people followed him trembling.*

Lesson Ten—The Journey to the Valley of Elah

On the seventh day, Saul grew tired of waiting for Samuel and offered a sacrifice to God. A sacrifice offered by anyone other than the priest was direct disobedience to God's clear command and was considered an effrontery to God. No sooner had he finished offering the sacrifice when Samuel arrived. King Saul was presumptuous in offering a sacrifice which should have been offered by Samuel.

1 Samuel 13:13–14

13 And Samuel said to Saul, Thou hast done foolishly: thou hast not kept the commandment of the Lord thy God, which he commanded thee: for now would the Lord have established thy kingdom upon Israel for ever.
14 But now thy kingdom shall not continue: the Lord hath sought him a man after his own heart, and the Lord hath commanded him to be captain over his people, because thou hast not kept that which the Lord commanded thee.

1 Samuel 15:26

26 And Samuel said unto Saul, I will not return with thee: for thou hast rejected the word of the Lord, and the Lord hath rejected thee from being king over Israel.

Because of Saul's behavior, God rejected him from being king. Now a new king would be chosen.

I. David's Calling

1 Samuel 16:7–13

7 But the Lord said unto Samuel, Look not on his countenance, or on the height of his stature; because I have refused him: for the Lord seeth not as man seeth; for man looketh on the outward appearance, but the Lord looketh on the heart.

9 Then Jesse made Shammah to pass by. And he said, Neither hath the LORD chosen this.

10 Again, Jesse made seven of his sons to pass before Samuel. And Samuel said unto Jesse, The LORD hath not chosen these.

11 And Samuel said unto Jesse, Are here all thy children? And he said, There remaineth yet the youngest, and, behold, he keepeth the sheep. And Samuel said unto Jesse, Send and fetch him: for we will not sit down till he come hither.

12 And he sent, and brought him in. Now he was ruddy, and withal of a beautiful countenance, and goodly to look to. And the LORD said, Arise, anoint him: for this is he.

13 Then Samuel took the horn of oil, and anointed him in the midst of his brethren: and the Spirit of the LORD came upon David from that day forward. So Samuel rose up, and went to Ramah.

A. *The purpose of David's calling*

God sent Samuel to the house of Jesse, for He had chosen among Jesse's sons the next king of Israel.

1 SAMUEL 16:1

1 And the LORD said unto Samuel, How long wilt thou mourn for Saul, seeing I have rejected him from reigning over Israel? fill thine horn with oil, and go, I will send thee to Jesse the Bethlehemite: for I have provided me a king among his sons.

There are two reasons why a new king was being chosen of the Lord. First, Saul was the king chosen of the people. The Scriptures record that the people demanded this king. He was a king of the people's will, not God's will.

Lesson Ten—The Journey to the Valley of Elah

1 Samuel 8:5

5 And said unto him, Behold, thou art old, and thy sons walk not in thy ways: now make us a king to judge us like all the nations.

1 Samuel 15:11

11 It repenteth me that I have set up Saul to be king: for he is turned back from following me, and hath not performed my commandments. And it grieved Samuel; and he cried unto the Lord all night.

Second, God was looking for a man after His own heart. David, God's choice for the next king, had a heart for God and a desire to know Him and obey all His commands. It was not his physical appearance, abilities, or talents that brought David favor with God; it was the condition of his heart. God is looking for the same attributes in Christians today. He is looking for someone who has a holy heart, filled with integrity, and who is willing to serve in whatever capacity He designs.

1 Samuel 16:7

7 But the Lord said unto Samuel, Look not on his countenance, or on the height of his stature; because I have refused him: for the Lord seeth not as man seeth; for man looketh on the outward appearance, but the Lord looketh on the heart.

1 Samuel 13:14

14 But now thy kingdom shall not continue: the Lord hath sought him a man after his own heart, and the Lord hath commanded him to be captain over his people, because thou hast not kept that which the Lord commanded thee.

David's heart in the twenty-third Psalm
- A Believing Heart—*"The Lord is My Shepherd"*

- A Teachable Heart—*"He maketh me to lie down in green pastures, he leadeth me beside the still waters"*
- A Holy Heart—*"he leadeth me in the paths of righteousness"*
- A Confident Heart—*"though I walk through the valley of the shadow of death, I will fear no evil."*
- A Thankful Heart—*"my cup runneth over"*
- A Fixed Heart—*"Surely goodness and mercy shall follow me all the days of my life"*

B. The process of David's calling

God guided Samuel through the process of selecting the next king. While Samuel looked on the outward appearance, God's selection was not based on physical attributes.

Jesse brought his sons before Samuel. When Samuel saw Eliab, he was sure that he would be the next king. After all, he looked like a king! But he was not the one. God rejected Eliab and warned Samuel not to look at the outward appearance. God was looking at the heart of the man, not at his height or countenance.

1 Samuel 16:7

7 But the Lord said unto Samuel, Look not on his countenance, or on the height of his stature; because I have refused him: for the Lord seeth not as man seeth; for man looketh on the outward appearance, but the Lord looketh on the heart.

Samuel went through the seven sons of Jesse, but God did not approve one! Then, Jesse remembered David, and they called for him.

Lesson Ten—The Journey to the Valley of Elah

1 Samuel 16:12

12 And he sent, and brought him in. Now he was ruddy, and withal of a beautiful countenance, and goodly to look to. And the LORD said, Arise, anoint him: for this is he.

God is looking for people with a heart for God and a desire to follow His Word in obedience.

Acts 13:22

22 And when he had removed him, he raised up unto them David to be their king; to whom also he gave testimony, and said, I have found David the son of Jesse, a man after mine own heart, which shall fulfil all my will.

Quote

Robert Murray McCheyne wrote to a missionary friend just after his friend had been ordained and said, "In great measure, according to the purity and perfections of the instrument, will be the success. It is not great talents God blesses so much as great likeness to Jesus. A holy minister is an awful weapon in the hand of God."

Not only do we see the selection of David, but we also see the sanctification of David in 1 Samuel 16:13.

1 Samuel 16:13

13 Then Samuel took the horn of oil, and anointed him in the midst of his brethren: and the Spirit of the LORD came upon David from that day forward. So Samuel rose up, and went to Ramah.

Samuel took the horn of oil and poured it over David's head, anointing him to be the next King of Israel. In the Old Testament, the oil was symbolic of the Holy Spirit coming upon an individual to anoint him with power, wisdom, and the ability to serve God. The anointing was symbolic of what was affirmed in David's life when the Scripture says, *"and the Spirit of the Lord came upon David from that day forward...."*

1 Samuel 16:18
18 Then answered one of the servants, and said, Behold, I have seen a son of Jesse the Bethlehemite, that is cunning in playing, and a mighty valiant man, and a man of war, and prudent in matters, and a comely person, and the Lord is with him.

God has also given us His Spirit (at salvation) to empower us for the work to which He has called each one of us. He comforts, directs, and strengthens our hearts. The Holy Spirit guides us into a life of holiness. God has given us the Holy Spirit to empower us for the work He has called us to do.

Ephesians 5:18
18 And be not drunk with wine, wherein is excess; but be filled with the Spirit;

Acts 1:8
8 But ye shall receive power, after that the Holy Ghost is come upon you: and ye shall be witnesses unto me both in Jerusalem, and in all Judaea, and in Samaria, and unto the uttermost part of the earth.

Although Samuel anointed David to be king that day, it would be many years before he actually took the throne. While David waited, he continued steadfast in watching his father's sheep and growing. His journey for the faith would prepare him to be king of Israel one day.

Lesson Ten—The Journey to the Valley of Elah

II. David's Cause

David's cause is revealed in 1 Samuel 17, when he fought against Goliath of Gath.

God had given David a cause to honor and glorify Him in all that he did. Along his journey, when David was still a young man, God proved his faith.

A. *His cause was for the faith.*

1 Samuel 17:1–8

1 Now the Philistines gathered together their armies to battle, and were gathered together at Shochoh, which belongeth to Judah, and pitched between Shochoh and Azekah, in Ephesdammim.

2 And Saul and the men of Israel were gathered together, and pitched by the valley of Elah, and set the battle in array against the Philistines.

3 And the Philistines stood on a mountain on the one side, and Israel stood on a mountain on the other side: and there was a valley between them.

4 And there went out a champion out of the camp of the Philistines, named Goliath, of Gath, whose height was six cubits and a span.

5 And he had an helmet of brass upon his head, and he was armed with a coat of mail; and the weight of the coat was five thousand shekels of brass.

6 And he had greaves of brass upon his legs, and a target of brass between his shoulders.

7 And the staff of his spear was like a weaver's beam; and his spear's head weighed six hundred shekels of iron: and one bearing a shield went before him.

8 And he stood and cried unto the armies of Israel, and said unto them, Why are ye come out to set your battle in array? am not I a Philistine, and ye servants to Saul? choose you a man for you, and let him come down to me.

1 Samuel 17:16

16 And the Philistine drew near morning and evening, and presented himself forty days.

In the verses listed above, we see the threat of the enemy. Israel, God's chosen people, and the Philistines were in a standoff. The Philistines were on one mountaintop and the Israelites were on the other. Each day, a giant Philistine, Goliath, would come out and challenge Israel to send a man to fight against him. God's army was petrified, obviously not trusting God to give them the victory. There is no indication that the army even sought God's help. They had become self-sufficient, just like their king. The army was unable to rout the enemy. They had forgotten that God was the one who would fight for them.

In 1 Samuel 17, we also see the concern of David. His older brothers were serving in Israel's army. So Jesse, David's father, sent him to check on his brothers and take supplies to them. When David reached the camp, he heard Goliath's challenge and watched as the army trembled. He was surprised to find that this Philistine defied the army of God and no one was troubled by it! David's only motivation was to defend God's honor. He did not look for recognition or praise. He aimed at nothing but the glory of God. David stood for God when no one else would. Are you willing to stand for God? We must live for His cause in this day!

1 Samuel 17:21–29

21 For Israel and the Philistines had put the battle in array, army against army.

Lesson Ten—The Journey to the Valley of Elah

22 And David left his carriage in the hand of the keeper of the carriage, and ran into the army, and came and saluted his brethren.

23 And as he talked with them, behold, there came up the champion, the Philistine of Gath, Goliath by name, out of the armies of the Philistines, and spake according to the same words: and David heard them.

24 And all the men of Israel, when they saw the man, fled from him, and were sore afraid.

25 And the men of Israel said, Have ye seen this man that is come up? surely to defy Israel is he come up: and it shall be, that the man who killeth him, the king will enrich him with great riches, and will give him his daughter, and make his father's house free in Israel.

26 And David spake to the men that stood by him, saying, What shall be done to the man that killeth this Philistine, and taketh away the reproach from Israel? for who is this uncircumcised Philistine, that he should defy the armies of the living God?

27 And the people answered him after this manner, saying, So shall it be done to the man that killeth him.

28 And Eliab his eldest brother heard when he spake unto the men; and Eliab's anger was kindled against David, and he said, Why camest thou down hither? and with whom hast thou left those few sheep in the wilderness? I know thy pride, and the naughtiness of thine heart; for thou art come down that thou mightest see the battle.

29 And David said, What have I now done? Is there not a cause?

2 Timothy 1:11–12

11 Whereunto I am appointed a preacher, and an apostle, and a teacher of the Gentiles.

12 For the which cause I also suffer these things: nevertheless I am not ashamed: for I know whom I have believed, and am persuaded that he is able to keep that which I have committed unto him against that day.

B. His cause was challenged. (v. 17:28)

David was criticized by his brother. Eliab questioned David's integrity, motive, and ability. He unjustly criticized David out of anger, accusing him of leaving his responsibilities unattended in order to see the battle. Meanwhile, Eliab had done nothing to defeat the enemy or defend the Lord.

> **Quote**
>
> Let the man who says it cannot be done not disturb the man doing it.—Chinese proverb

David was also challenged by Saul. Saul doubted David's ability, stating he was just a youth. David was probably somewhere between the ages of twelve and seventeen. He was a youth, but God still wanted to use him to defeat Goliath who was over nine feet tall, having a spear that weighted 65 pounds!

1 Samuel 17:31–33

31 And when the words were heard which David spake, they rehearsed them before Saul: and he sent for him.
32 And David said to Saul, Let no man's heart fail because of him; thy servant will go and fight with this Philistine.
33 And Saul said to David, Thou art not able to go against this Philistine to fight with him: for thou art but a youth, and he a man of war from his youth.

Both men, Eliab and Saul, forgot one thing: the Lord God of Israel!

III. David's Conflict

It is inevitable that we will face battles. Some will be daunting and seem like giants, yet our true character is shown when we face overwhelming circumstances.

A. David's preparation for battle

David was prepared by engaging in previous battles. His encounter with the lion and with the bear prepared him for his encounter with Goliath.

1 SAMUEL 17:33–37

33 And Saul said to David, Thou art not able to go against this Philistine to fight with him: for thou art but a youth, and he a man of war from his youth.
34 And David said unto Saul, Thy servant kept his father's sheep, and there came a lion, and a bear, and took a lamb out of the flock:
35 And I went out after him, and smote him, and delivered it out of his mouth: and when he arose against me, I caught him by his beard, and smote him, and slew him.
36 Thy servant slew both the lion and the bear: and this uncircumcised Philistine shall be as one of them, seeing he hath defied the armies of the living God.
37 David said moreover, The LORD that delivered me out of the paw of the lion, and out of the paw of the bear, he will deliver me out of the hand of this Philistine. And Saul said unto David, Go, and the LORD be with thee.

God uses every battle and trial in our lives to prepare us for greater usefulness. David had learned to trust in God along his journey. God strengthened David to kill a bear and a lion while he was protecting his father's sheep. He knew his own weaknesses and learned to depend fully on God's strength to be made perfect in those weaknesses.

David was also prepared with proven methods. While Saul encouraged David to use his military armor, David chose to stick with what was proven in his life. His sling had been with him as a shepherd boy on a hill. He knew it was trustworthy.

1 Samuel 17:38–40

38 And Saul armed David with his armour, and he put an helmet of brass upon his head; also he armed him with a coat of mail.
39 And David girded his sword upon his armour, and he assayed to go; for he had not proved it. And David said unto Saul, I cannot go with these; for I have not proved them. And David put them off him.
40 And he took his staff in his hand, and chose him five smooth stones out of the brook, and put them in a shepherd's bag which he had, even in a scrip; and his sling was in his hand: and he drew near to the Philistine.

God has proven methods for the Christian life. The Bible is full of instructions for the church and for our homes. And God's methods are always best.

1 Corinthians 1:27–29

27 But God hath chosen the foolish things of the world to confound the wise; and God hath chosen the weak things of the world to confound the things which are mighty;

28 And base things of the world, and things which are despised, hath God chosen, yea, and things which are not, to bring to nought things that are:
29 That no flesh should glory in his presence.

B. David's power in battle

Goliath was the best man the world could produce in weaponry and in advantage. The world may always seem to have the advantage with more intelligence and stronger might. On the surface, it often looks like Satan's Goliaths will prevail against God's people. But with God, all things are possible! We simply need to take Him at His Word and trust Him.

PHILIPPIANS 4:13
13 I can do all things through Christ which strengtheneth me.

David's power in battle came from his trust in the Lord. He was confident that God would work on his behalf to conquer the enemy.

When David was first anointed, even Samuel did not think David would be the one chosen to be king. His brothers ridiculed him when he went to the battlefield. Even the king of the land doubted that he could defeat the giant. David knew, though, that he was not in charge. The Lord was the one fighting the battle, and He could be trusted for the power and the victory.

1 SAMUEL 17:45–47
45 Then said David to the Philistine, Thou comest to me with a sword, and with a spear, and with a shield: but I come to thee in the name of the LORD of hosts, the God of the armies of Israel, whom thou hast defied.

46 This day will the Lord deliver thee into mine hand; and I will smite thee, and take thine head from thee; and I will give the carcases of the host of the Philistines this day unto the fowls of the air, and to the wild beasts of the earth; that all the earth may know that there is a God in Israel.
47 And all this assembly shall know that the Lord saveth not with sword and spear: for the battle is the Lord's, and he will give you into our hands.

David's power in battle was also a result of his desire to glorify God. His passion for God was undaunted by disapproval, ridicule, or fear. He was so focused on God and giving Him the glory that it did not matter what others thought.

His confidence in God's care and strength was so intense that he was valiant in his stand for God. David made it clear that Goliath had defied Israel's God by mocking His armies and that now he would feel the sting of God's might. If you were on the hill overlooking the valley of Elah, would you have been trembling with the army of Israel or standing side by side with David?

Zechariah 4:6
6 Then he answered and spake unto me, saying, This is the word of the Lord unto Zerubbabel, saying, Not by might, nor by power, but by my spirit, saith the Lord of hosts.

C. David's prevailing in battle

1 Samuel 17:48–51
48 And it came to pass, when the Philistine arose, and came and drew nigh to meet David, that David hasted, and ran toward the army to meet the Philistine.

Lesson Ten—The Journey to the Valley of Elah

49 And David put his hand in his bag, and took thence a stone, and slang it, and smote the Philistine in his forehead, that the stone sunk into his forehead; and he fell upon his face to the earth.
50 So David prevailed over the Philistine with a sling and with a stone, and smote the Philistine, and slew him; but there was no sword in the hand of David.
51 Therefore David ran, and stood upon the Philistine, and took his sword, and drew it out of the sheath thereof, and slew him, and cut off his head therewith. And when the Philistines saw their champion was dead, they fled.

Goliath arose (and "Goliaths" will arise in our lives, too). But the moment David saw Goliath move, he began to run toward the giant. With five smooth stones and a slingshot, David defeated the giant that day. God's power was upon him as he stood for God, and God's strength was demonstrated through his life. It doesn't matter to God how many men He has for the battle, because the victory is not dependent upon man's power but God's.

Is there a giant in your life? Do you struggle with defeat as you face it? Like David, claim God's power to prevail against the giants in your life. We serve the same God that David did, and He will always prove Himself faithful.

Psalm 115:1–3

1 Not unto us, O Lord, not unto us, but unto thy name give glory, for thy mercy, and for thy truth's sake.
2 Wherefore should the heathen say, Where is now their God?
3 But our God is in the heavens: he hath done whatsoever he hath pleased.

Matthew 19:26

26 But Jesus beheld them, and said unto them, With men this is impossible; but with God all things are possible.

Conclusion

David's journey for the faith showed that he desired to serve God above all else. He spent time as a shepherd getting to know God, and he was familiar with His ways. He was a man after God's own heart and was committed to his God-given cause.

Just like David, we will all face giants on our journeys. We may feel outmanned, overwhelmed, or defeated. But God is with us every step of the way. He stands ready to provide the strength and power needed for victory.

And may we also find hope in the promise that Jesus is coming soon!

Isaiah 11:1–3

1 And there shall come forth a rod out of the stem of Jesse, and a Branch shall grow out of his roots:

2 And the spirit of the Lord shall rest upon him, the spirit of wisdom and understanding, the spirit of counsel and might, the spirit of knowledge and of the fear of the Lord;

3 And shall make him of quick understanding in the fear of the Lord: and he shall not judge after the sight of his eyes, neither reprove after the hearing of his ears:

Lesson Ten—The Journey to the Valley of Elah

Study Questions

1. According to Acts 13:22, how was David's heart described?
   David was a man after God's own heart. His heart was like God's.

   ACTS 13:22
   22 And when he had removed him, he raised up unto them David to be their king; to whom also he gave testimony, and said, I have found David the son of Jesse, a man after mine own heart, which shall fulfil all my will.

2. As Samuel looked at Jesse's sons, which one did he think would be the next king?
   Looking on the outward appearance, Samuel thought Eliab would be the king to follow Saul.

3. According to 1 Samuel 16:7, when God looks at us, what does He see?
   When God sees man, He see the heart.

   1 SAMUEL 16:7
   7 But the LORD said unto Samuel, Look not on his countenance, or on the height of his stature; because I have refused him: for the LORD seeth not as man seeth; for man looketh on the outward appearance, but the LORD looketh on the heart.

4. In the Old Testament, what did the anointing of oil symbolize?
   In the Old Testament, the anointing of oil symbolized the empowering of the Holy Spirit.

5. Read 2 Timothy 1:11–12. Here, Paul states his call and his cause. Briefly explain how these verses can also describe the calling and cause of David.

   2 Timothy 1:11–12
   11 Whereunto I am appointed a preacher, and an apostle, and a teacher of the Gentiles.
   12 For the which cause I also suffer these things: nevertheless I am not ashamed: for I know whom I have believed, and am persuaded that he is able to keep that which I have committed unto him against that day.

   David was called and anointed of God to be the next king of Israel. He was to be the teacher of God's ways and was to lead God's people. That was his cause: to declare and defend the faith that was given to him by God and to glorify God in the process.

6. Name two people who challenged David's cause.
   David's brother Eliab and King Saul both challenged David's cause.

7. What experiences prepared David for battle against Goliath?
   David killed a lion and a bear with his sling, preparing him to fight against Goliath.

Memory Verse

Hebrews 4:16
16 Let us therefore come boldly unto the throne of grace, that we may obtain mercy, and find grace to help in time of need.

LESSON ELEVEN

The Journey to Zion

Key Verses

1 Samuel 18:1–9; 2 Samuel 11–12

Lesson Overview

As Christians, we will face trials and temptations on our journeys of faith. David faced an intense trial for an extended period when King Saul was trying to kill him. His response to the trial is an example for us to follow. Later, when David became king, he faced a great temptation and chose to sin. Throughout this lesson, we examine David's life, the consequences of his sin, and the steps he followed to restore his fellowship with a holy God.

Lesson Aim

We want to impress upon the student the importance of staying focused on God during times of trial and fleeing Satan during times of temptation. When we fall during one of these times, we can experience triumph when we confess our sin to the Lord.

Lesson Goals

At the conclusion of this lesson, students should:
- Seek the Lord in response to trials.
- Find rest in God when discouraged and weary.

- Flee when faced with temptation.
- Understand the consequences of sinning against God.
- Learn to confess sin in order to experience victory through Christ.

Teaching Outline

I. David's Great Trial
   A. The reason for the trial
      1. David's popularity
      2. Saul's problem
   B. The response to the trial
   C. His rest in the trial

II. David's Great Temptation
   A. David's lapse
   B. David's lust
      1. His look
      2. His lust
      3. His pride
   C. David's losses
      1. Fellowship with the Lord
      2. Following of the family

III. David's Triumph
   A. A righteous confrontation
   B. A real confession
   C. A restored kingdom

LESSON ELEVEN

The Journey to Zion

Text

1 Samuel 18:1–9; 2 Samuel 11–12

Introduction

A valiant, intrepid soldier during America's War for Independence sought only glory for himself and quickly rose in rank in the service of America. During the first three years of battle, this ardent patriot distinguished himself and gained appointment as a brigadier general. He was a pompous, extravagant, egocentric man who craved power and wealth and would do anything necessary to promote himself. His actions often bordered on insubordination. He was ruthless, willing to risk his life and the lives of others to get what he wanted.

When American commander General Horatio Gates relieved Benedict Arnold of his command during the battle of Saratoga, Benedict Arnold's anger and jealousy worsened. Becoming a bitter, jealous man, he found himself in financial ruin, facing a court martial. Benedict Arnold then made a fateful decision to seek fortune and fame working against America in the service of Great Britain. His jealousy of others eventually led him to betray West Point in an act of treason against his country. Hated in America and disdained in Great Britain, Benedict Arnold's name is still synonymous with treachery and treason.

Sin will take us farther than we want to go! Benedict Arnold's pride led him to betray his own country. In our story today, we will see that Saul's jealously led to cruel behavior, and David's failure to go to battle (as he was supposed to) led to adultery.

In last week's lesson, The Journey to Elah, we saw David's anointing and victory over Goliath. Today, we learn about David's journey to Zion.

Zion is the word for Jerusalem. After David became the king, he moved the capital from Hebron to Jerusalem. Here, in the middle of David's life, we see some of the great tragedies and triumphs of a man of God.

I. David's Great Trial

David's great trial during this time in his life was that of Saul's relentless pursuit of him. From the time that David played the harp for Saul until Saul's death, the king sought to kill David. The Bible gives us greater insight into David's trial.

1 SAMUEL 18:10–12

10 And it came to pass on the morrow, that the evil spirit from God came upon Saul, and he prophesied in the midst of the

Lesson Eleven—The Journey to Zion

house: and David played with his hand, as at other times: and there was a javelin in Saul's hand.

11 And Saul cast the javelin; for he said, I will smite David even to the wall with it. And David avoided out of his presence twice.

12 And Saul was afraid of David, because the LORD was with him, and was departed from Saul.

A. *The reason for the trial*

1 SAMUEL 18:6–9

6 And it came to pass as they came, when David was returned from the slaughter of the Philistine, that the women came out of all cities of Israel, singing and dancing, to meet king Saul, with tabrets, with joy, and with instruments of musick.

7 And the women answered one another as they played, and said, Saul hath slain his thousands, and David his ten thousands.

8 And Saul was very wroth, and the saying displeased him; and he said, They have ascribed unto David ten thousands, and to me they have ascribed but thousands: and what can he have more but the kingdom?

9 And Saul eyed David from that day and forward.

These verses give record of David's increasing popularity. He was lovingly accepted among the people of Israel.

1 SAMUEL 18:16

16 But all Israel and Judah loved David, because he went out and came in before them.

Through his many victories in battle, David became a hero in Israel. The children of Israel sang David's praises.

David was not simply gaining the favor of Israel, however. He also obtained the favor of the Lord during this time (1 Samuel 18:12).

David's increased popularity revealed Saul's heart problem. First of all, Saul's problem involved jealousy. When the women of the city cheered, "Saul has slain his thousands, but David his ten thousands," Saul thought that the praise people were giving to David belonged to him, and jealousy gripped his heart.

One of the greatest mistakes Christians make is comparing themselves with other Christians. Sometimes, as people sit in church, the devil tells them that they don't belong or that they are not perfect enough. May we learn from the life of Saul the need to overcome jealously and comparison.

Illustration

Two cows were grazing in a pasture when they saw a milk truck pass. On the side of the truck were the words, "Pasteurized, homogenized, standardized, vitamin A added."

One cow sighed and said to the other, "Makes you feel sort of inadequate, doesn't it?"

Saul's problem of fear is also revealed in his dealings with David. Saul saw that God was with David and that he behaved himself wisely; thus, Saul was afraid.

1 Samuel 18:12

12 And **Saul was afraid of David,** because the Lord was with him, and was departed from Saul.

Lesson Eleven—The Journey to Zion

1 Samuel 18:15

15 Wherefore when Saul saw that he behaved himself very wisely, **he was afraid of him.**

B. The response to the trial

Because of Saul's jealously, David had to flee. He knew it would be wrong to fight against the king whom God had chosen.

1 Samuel 19:10

10 And Saul sought to smite David even to the wall with the javelin; but he slipped away out of Saul's presence, and he smote the javelin into the wall: and David fled, and escaped that night.

After David fled from the presence of Saul, he eventually sought refuge in the cave of Adullam and hid there. While he was hiding from Saul, many who were distressed came to him.

1 Samuel 22:1–2

1 David therefore departed thence, and escaped to the cave Adullam: and when his brethren and all his father's house heard it, they went down thither to him.
2 And every one that was in distress, and every one that was in debt, and every one that was discontented, gathered themselves unto him; and he became a captain over them: and there were with him about four hundred men.

Eventually, David became discouraged in his trial. Notice what he said in his heart in these verses:

1 Samuel 27:1–2

1 And David said in his heart, I shall now perish one day by the hand of Saul: there is nothing better for me than

that I should speedily escape into the land of the Philistines; and Saul shall despair of me, to seek me any more in any coast of Israel: so shall I escape out of his hand.
2 And David arose, and he passed over with the six hundred men that were with him unto Achish, the son of Maoch, king of Gath.

Illustration

Sal claims it wasn't intentional, but his wife couldn't help but wonder if his spelling was somehow affected by subconscious marital discouragement. On the card he gave Miriam, Sal misspelled "milestone" and wrote, "Our 40th anniversary is a real millstone."

C. His rest in the trial

While his friend Jonathan and his wife Michal helped to protect him as he fled, David's ultimate hope was in the Lord. Yes, he was hiding from Saul in the wilderness, and yes, he was discouraged. But he came to the point where he found rest in the Lord.

After a trying time in a place called Ziklag, David encouraged himself in the Lord and in God's plan for him.

1 Samuel 30:6

6 And David was greatly distressed; for the people spake of stoning him, because the soul of all the people was grieved, every man for his sons and for his daughters: but David encouraged himself in the Lord his God.

God led David and never forsook him through any of his difficulties. He found great rest in the Lord.

Lesson Eleven—The Journey to Zion

1 Corinthians 10:13

13 There hath no temptation taken you but such as is common to man: but God is faithful, who will not suffer you to be tempted above that ye are able; but will with the temptation also make a way to escape, that ye may be able to bear it.

II. David's Great Temptation

After King Saul was killed in battle, David, Israel's hero, began to reign as king over all Israel. David was still a man after God's own heart. He desired more than anything else to serve and honor God. His greatest ambition was not to be king, but to be greatly used by God.

2 Samuel 5:3–4

3 So all the elders of Israel came to the king to Hebron; and king David made a league with them in Hebron before the Lord: and they anointed David king over Israel.

4 David was thirty years old when he began to reign, and he reigned forty years.

The children of Israel still had many enemies to defeat and many battles to fight. David led the people as he followed God, and God gave victory after victory. It was during this time when David faced a great temptation to do evil.

2 Samuel 11:1–5

1 And it came to pass, after the year was expired, at the time when kings go forth to battle, that David sent Joab, and his servants with him, and all Israel; and they destroyed the children of Ammon, and besieged Rabbah. But David tarried still at Jerusalem.

2 And it came to pass in an eveningtide, that David arose from off his bed, and walked upon the roof of the king's house: and from the roof he saw a woman washing herself; and the woman was very beautiful to look upon.
3 And David sent and enquired after the woman. And one said, Is not this Bathsheba, the daughter of Eliam, the wife of Uriah the Hittite?
4 And David sent messengers, and took her; and she came in unto him, and he lay with her; for she was purified from her uncleanness: and she returned unto her house.
5 And the woman conceived, and sent and told David, and said, I am with child.

A. David's lapse

It was the set time every year that the kings and nations would go to war, yet David *"tarried still at Jerusalem"* (2 Samuel 11:1). When we are out of the way of our duty, we are in the way of temptation.

B. David's lust

Quote

"Idleness gives great advantage to the tempter. Standing waters gather filth. The bed of sloth often proves the bed of lust."—Matthew Henry

Notice the next stages of this horrible event (2 Samuel 11:2–5):

1. His look

David saw a woman washing herself. The sin came in to David's life by way of the eye. He was tempted, as was Eve in Genesis, by what he saw.

2. His lust

2 Samuel 11:3–4

3 And David sent and enquired after the woman. And one said, Is not this Bathsheba, the daughter of Eliam, the wife of Uriah the Hittite?

4 And David sent messengers, and took her; and she came in unto him, and he lay with her; for she was purified from her uncleanness: and she returned unto her house.

Quote

Christians often want to retreat from the spiritual battle and the war that rages, forgetting they will always find us. Better to be weary in the battle than to become apathetic, lazy, and caught off guard.

1 Peter 5:8

8 Be sober, be vigilant; because your adversary the devil, as a roaring lion, walketh about, seeking whom he may devour:

3. His pride

Through pride and deceit, David attempted to hide his sin. Sending a message, David commanded that Uriah be placed in the front of the battle line where he was sure to be killed.

2 Samuel 11:15–17

15 And he wrote in the letter, saying, Set ye Uriah in the forefront of the hottest battle, and retire ye from him, that he may be smitten, and die.

16 And it came to pass, when Joab observed the city, that he assigned Uriah unto a place where he knew that valiant men were.

17 And the men of the city went out, and fought with Joab: and there fell some of the people of the servants of David; and Uriah the Hittite died also.

When David received the message that Uriah was indeed dead, he married Bathsheba. But the man who was once known as a man after God's own heart was now a man who grieved God's heart.

2 Samuel 11:26–27

26 And when the wife of Uriah heard that Uriah her husband was dead, she mourned for her husband.
27 And when the mourning was past, David sent and fetched her to his house, and she became his wife, and bare him a son. But the thing that David had done displeased the LORD.

Illustration

Gary Richmond, a former zoo keeper, had this to say: Raccoons go through a glandular change at about twenty-four months. After that they often attack their owners. Since a thirty-pound raccoon can be equal to a one-hundred-pound dog in a scrap, I felt compelled to mention the change coming to a pet raccoon owned by a young friend of mine, Julie. She listened politely as I explained the coming danger. I'll never forget her answer. "It will be different for me...." And she smiled as she added, "Bandit wouldn't hurt me. He just wouldn't." Three months later, Julie underwent plastic surgery for facial lacerations sustained when her adult raccoon attacked her for no apparent reason. Bandit was released into the wild. Sin, too, often comes dressed in an adorable guise, and as we play with it, how easy it is to say, "It will be different for me." The results are predictable.

C. David's losses

David suffered great and personal losses because of his sin. The greatest loss was that of his fellowship with the Lord (2 Samuel 11:26–27).

David also suffered severe consequences in his family life. Notice the tragic events that came as a result of David's sin.

- The Death of the Infant—2 Samuel 12:15–18
- Amnon (David's Son) rapes Tamar —2 Samuel 13:1–12
- Amnon Killed By Absolom—2 Samuel 13:29
- Absolom is killed by Joab—2 Samuel 18:10–12
- Amasa (David's Nephew) was killed by Joab —2 Samuel 20:9–10

2 Samuel 12:14

14 Howbeit, because by this deed thou hast given great occasion to the enemies of the Lord to blaspheme, the child also that is born unto thee shall surely die.

Galatians 6:7–8

7 Be not deceived; God is not mocked: for whatsoever a man soweth, that shall he also reap.
8 For he that soweth to his flesh shall of the flesh reap corruption; but he that soweth to the Spirit shall of the Spirit reap life everlasting.

Along our journeys of faith, we will have trials and temptations. Both are inevitable. To continue advancing on our journeys of faith, we must respond by fleeing temptation and trusting God during times of trial.

III. David's Triumph

Though David suffered immensely because of his sin, he was able to experience triumph once again. God gives record of this portion of David's journey in 2 Samuel 12.

A. *A righteous confrontation*

God sent the prophet Nathan to expose David's sin. By recounting an illustration about two men, the first owned one little ewe lamb and the other possessed many sheep, Nathan confronted King David with his sin.

God's mercy was evident in David's life at this point, because, according to the law, David deserved to die.

2 Samuel 12:1–6

1   And the Lord sent Nathan unto David. And he came unto him, and said unto him, There were two men in one city; the one rich, and the other poor.
2   The rich man had exceeding many flocks and herds:
3   But the poor man had nothing, save one little ewe lamb, which he had bought and nourished up: and it grew up together with him, and with his children; it did eat of his own meat, and drank of his own cup, and lay in his bosom, and was unto him as a daughter.
4   And there came a traveller unto the rich man, and he spared to take of his own flock and of his own herd, to dress for the wayfaring man that was come unto him; but took the poor man's lamb, and dressed it for the man that was come to him.
5   And David's anger was greatly kindled against the man; and he said to Nathan, As the Lord liveth, the man that hath done this thing shall surely die:
6   And he shall restore the lamb fourfold, because he did this thing, and because he had no pity.

Nathan proceeds to tell David that he is the man referred to in his story.

2 Samuel 12:7–9
7 And Nathan said to David, **Thou art the man.** Thus saith the Lord God of Israel, I anointed thee king over Israel, and I delivered thee out of the hand of Saul;
8 And I gave thee thy master's house, and thy master's wives into thy bosom, and gave thee the house of Israel and of Judah; and if that had been too little, I would moreover have given unto thee such and such things.
9 Wherefore hast thou despised the commandment of the Lord, to do evil in his sight? thou hast killed Uriah the Hittite with the sword, and hast taken his wife to be thy wife, and hast slain him with the sword of the children of Ammon.

B. *A real confession*

2 Samuel 12:13–14
13 And David said unto Nathan, I have sinned against the Lord. And Nathan said unto David, The Lord also hath put away thy sin; thou shalt not die.
14 Howbeit, because by this deed thou hast given great occasion to the enemies of the Lord to blaspheme, the child also that is born unto thee shall surely die.

Nathan exposed King David's sin and called for David's repentance. With a broken heart, David confessed, repented, and sought God's restoration penning his thoughts in Psalm 51.

Psalm 51:3–4
3 For I acknowledge my transgressions: and my sin is ever before me.

4 Against thee, thee only, have I sinned, and done this evil in thy sight: that thou mightest be justified when thou speakest, and be clear when thou judgest.

C. A restored kingdom

God preserved David's life and continued his kingdom.

2 SAMUEL 22:1–4

1 And David spake unto the LORD the words of this song in the day that the LORD had delivered him out of the hand of all his enemies, and out of the hand of Saul:
2 And he said, The LORD is my rock, and my fortress, and my deliverer;
3 The God of my rock; in him will I trust: he is my shield, and the horn of my salvation, my high tower, and my refuge, my saviour; thou savest me from violence.
4 I will call on the LORD, who is worthy to be praised: so shall I be saved from mine enemies.

Conclusion

Three words summarize David's journey to Zion:

- Trial—Saul
- Temptation—Bathsheba
- Triumph—Repentance

May we learn this: In our trials, seek the Lord. In our temptations, flee Satan!

Lesson Eleven—The Journey to Zion

Study Questions

1. What was David's initial response to his trial with Saul?
   David fled and became discouraged before finding comfort and rest in the Lord.

2. Read 1 Samuel 30:1–6. David was still enduring a great trial and had just experienced defeat at the hand of the Amalekites, yet what did he do in 1 Samuel 30:6?
   David encouraged himself in the Lord. He found rest during his trial.

3. Think of a trial you may have experienced in the past or perhaps are enduring now. Explain how you handled or are handling your trial and identify key moments when you encouraged yourself in the Lord. If you have not found rest in the Lord, spend a moment now to encourage yourself in Him.
   Answers will vary as to personal experience.

4. Explain David's lapse as recorded in 2 Samuel 11:1.
   When the other kings went to battle, David tarried at home.

5. While David's trial dealt with his relationship to Saul, whom did his temptation involve?
   David's temptation was with Bethsheba.

6. What should a Christian do when faced with temptation?
   The Bible commands us to flee temptation.

7. Look up the following verses and list the consequences David experienced as a result of his sin:

   2 Samuel 12:15–16
   2 Samuel 13:1–12
   2 Samuel 13:29
   2 Samuel 18:10–12

   The Death of the Infant—2 Samuel 12:15–16
   Amnon (David's Son) rapes Tamar—2 Samuel 13:1–12
   Amnon Killed By Absolom—2 Samuel 13:29
   Absolom is killed by Joab—2 Samuel 18:10–12

8. What did David do to experience triumph after his temptation?
   David confessed his sin to the Lord and repented of his wrongdoing.

Memory Verse

1 Corinthians 10:13

13 There hath no temptation taken you but such as is common to man: but God is faithful, who will not suffer you to be tempted above that ye are able; but will with the temptation also make a way to escape, that ye may be able to bear it.

LESSON TWELVE

The Journey to the Cross

Key Verses
John 17

Lesson Overview
The most significant journey recorded in the Bible is the journey to the Cross. Jesus' journey to Golgotha was incredibly personal and painful. Yet His journey was wonderfully powerful, as He ultimately conquered death and the grave in an expression of love for mankind. This power is still changing lives today.

As Christians, we must constantly examine our lives in light of Bible truth. By considering the people and events surrounding Jesus' death on the Cross, we can develop an understanding of the significance of Jesus' death, burial, and resurrection. We must evaluate our spiritual journeys in light of these truths, beginning with the confidence of salvation and continuing forward in a life of righteous living.

Lesson Aim
We must realize that if Christ died for us, we should accept His gift of salvation and then determine to live our lives in a way that would glorify Him.

Lesson Goals

At the conclusion of this lesson, students should:
- Cultivate a heart of gratitude for the work Jesus accomplished on the Cross.
- Strive to glorify God in all areas of life.
- Determine to stand with God, rather than stand with those who would deny and betray Him.
- Accept the gift of eternal life, if they have not done so already.
- Acknowledge God's purpose for their lives and seek to fulfill it.

Teaching Outline

I. A Planned Journey
    A. A personal journey
        1. Planned between the Father and the Son
        2. Planned before the world was known
    B. A purposeful journey
        1. To give eternal life
        2. To glorify God

II. A Painful Journey
    A. Personal betrayal
        1. Betrayed by Judas
        2. Denied by Peter
    B. Physical beating

III. A Powerful Journey
    A. The power of love
    B. The power of humility
        1. Crucified between two thieves
        2. Offered forgiveness
    C. The power of redemption
        1. The payment was made.
        2. Atonement was accomplished.

LESSON TWELVE

The Journey to the Cross

Text

JOHN 17

Introduction

The United States Patent Office, opened in 1790, issued its first patent to Samuel Hopkins. The patent for "new apparatus" for making Potash was signed by President George Washington. Three other patents were granted that year. Since that time, the United States Patent Office has granted over 6 million patents to worthy inventors. (Some more creative patents include a screen door for a submarine, a lead balloon, and a drive thru ATM machine with instructions written in Braille!) Each of these devices represents a moment when an idea was born in the mind of the inventor. Each patent represents an idea that occurred—a light that suddenly dawned that could solve an age-old problem.

Has it ever occurred to you that nothing has ever occurred to God? He is omniscient, which means He is all knowing. He is not startled by events that are happening in the world today, because He has always known what was coming. Acts 15:18 bears record of this truth, *"Known unto God are all his works from the beginning of the world."*

John 17 is one of the great prayers recorded in the Bible. Jesus, in His omniscience, knew the journey to the Cross was upon Him. This journey was planned before the beginning of time to save the souls of those who believe in Him, yet it involved personal betrayal and immense physical pain.

Jesus entered Jerusalem in triumph, but was rejected by the Jewish leaders. He cleansed the temple and gave the Olivet discourse. He ate the Passover meal and walked to the Valley of Kidron. Here, Jesus prayed to His Father for Himself and then for His disciples.

I. A Planned Journey

The crucifixion and its surrounding events were pre-ordained by God before time began. Jesus began His prayer (in John 17) by acknowledging this hour had come.

A. A personal journey

JOHN 17:1–4

1 *These words spake Jesus, and lifted up his eyes to heaven, and said, Father, the hour is come; glorify thy Son, that thy Son also may glorify thee:*

> **TEACHING TIP**
>
> *John 17 is often referred to as the High Priestly Prayer of Christ.*

Lesson Twelve—The Journey to the Cross

2 As thou hast given him power over all flesh, that he should give eternal life to as many as thou hast given him.
3 And this is life eternal, that they might know thee the only true God, and Jesus Christ, whom thou hast sent.
4 I have glorified thee on the earth: I have finished the work which thou gavest me to do.

This personal journey was planned between God the Father and God the Son. John 17:1 indicates that Jesus acknowledged the plan to His Father, "*These words spake Jesus, and lifted up his eyes to heaven, and said, Father, the hour is come; glorify thy Son, that thy Son also may glorify thee:*"

The journey was also planned before the world was known. Before the foundations of the world were created—before "the world was"—the Father had planned this journey to the Cross to become the satisfactory payment for the sins of mankind. John 17:5 records this truth, as it states, "*And now, O Father, glorify thou me with thine own self with the glory which I had with thee before the world was.*"

Jesus is eternal God! Before time came into existence, the virgin birth was planned, His earthly ministry was foreordained, and His journey to the Cross was predestined.

John 1:1–2
1 In the beginning was the Word, and the Word was with God, and the Word was God.
2 The same was in the beginning with God.

1 Peter 1:18–20
18 Forasmuch as ye know that ye were not redeemed with corruptible things, as silver and gold, from your vain conversation received by tradition from your fathers;

19 But with the precious blood of Christ, as of a lamb without blemish and without spot:
20 Who verily was foreordained before the foundation of the world, but was manifest in these last times for you,

B. *A purposeful journey*

The journey to the Cross served two primary purposes. The first purpose was to give eternal life. What an amazing and wonderful purpose! Because He was willing to give His life, we are able to experience eternal life in Heaven.

1 John 5:20
20 And we know that the Son of God is come, and hath given us an understanding, that we may know him that is true, and we are in him that is true, even in his Son Jesus Christ. This is the true God, and eternal life.

The second purpose of His death on the Cross was to glorify God. Jesus said in John 17:4, "*I have glorified thee on the earth: I have finished the work which thou gavest me to do.*" We see a second reference to the glory of the Father in John 12:23, as it states, "*And Jesus answered them, saying, The hour is come, that the Son of man should be glorified.*" In both instances, Jesus linked the glorification of God with the crucifixion.

God was glorified through Jesus' painful journey to the Cross. Jesus allowed God to accomplish His eternal purposes through Him. Jesus lived His life on earth aware of and focused on God's mission for Him. Are you focused on God's eternal purposes for your life? Are you accomplishing those purposes in a way that glorifies God?

Lesson Twelve—The Journey to the Cross

1 Corinthians 6:20

20 *For ye are bought with a price: therefore glorify God in your body, and in your spirit, which are God's.*

II. A Painful Journey

The journey to the Cross took Jesus through the Garden of Gethsamene and up Golgotha's Hill, where He experienced unbelievable pain.

A. *Personal betrayal*

John 18:1

1 *When Jesus had spoken these words, he went forth with his disciples over the brook Cedron, where was a garden, into the which he entered, and his disciples.*

God uses people in the Bible to illustrate different aspects of our journeys of faith. Some characters exemplify a model to follow while others demonstrate characteristics to avoid. Nevertheless, every example given in Scripture is for our edification. Two men in this story provide characteristics to avoid on our journeys of faith.

Jesus experienced personal betrayal from a man named Judas. The Bible says in John 18:5 that Judas stood with the men who had come for Jesus.

John 18:5

5 *They answered him, Jesus of Nazareth. Jesus saith unto them, I am he. And Judas also, which betrayed him, stood with them.*

Judas arrived with a band of Roman soldiers, perhaps the guard of the Sanhedrin, and stood with them.

He stood with Satan. Judas outwardly appeared to be as one of the disciples, but Jesus knew his heart.

MATTHEW 26:48
48 Now he that betrayed him gave them a sign, saying, Whomsoever I shall kiss, that same is he: hold him fast.

Judas labored side by side with the other disciples, but He betrayed Jesus. He was not a true disciple.

As members of a church, some people walk, talk, and act like Christians, but they have never received Jesus as their Saviour. Judas walked, talked, and pretended to be a disciple, but he never truly believed Jesus was God. Are you sure that you are a Christian? Is your life free from pretense? May we avoid "acting" like Christians when our hearts would reveal otherwise.

Another disciple, Peter, was there that night also. He was hiding out, warming his hands with those who were seeking to kill Jesus. He stood with the wrong crowd, and his fear caused him to deny Christ. In the upper room, Peter had boasted that he would not deny the Lord! Matthew 26:33–34 says, *"Peter answered and said unto him, Though all men shall be offended because of thee, yet will I never be offended. Jesus said unto him, Verily I say unto thee, That this night, before the cock crow, thou shalt deny me thrice."* The Bible records the denial of Peter, who also "stood with them"—the officers and servants—in the following verses:

JOHN 18:17–18
17 Then saith the damsel that kept the door unto Peter, Art not thou also one of this man's disciples? He saith, I am not.

Lesson Twelve—The Journey to the Cross

18 And the servants and officers stood there, who had made a fire of coals; for it was cold: and they warmed themselves: and Peter stood with them, and warmed himself.

Peter was recognized three different times, yet each time Peter denied that he knew Jesus. He did not want to be identified with Jesus Christ.

Peter is a picture of a Christian who is ashamed to be identified with Christ. He journeyed daily with Jesus when the miracles and blessings were evident. Nevertheless, Peter allowed his fear to bring about his denial of Jesus.

Many Christians today are seeking to blend in with the lost world around them. Rather than standing for God and identifying with Christ, they choose to deny Him. May the example of Peter remind us to stand up for Jesus. May we not cause grief to our Saviour by choosing to deny Him in our society today.

B. *Physical beating*

The angry mob had taken Jesus to Pilate, who was Caesar's representative in Judea. Pilate found no fault in Jesus. Yet, the physical beating endured by Jesus is almost beyond comprehension. He was treated unfairly and cruelly.

> **Scourge** (noun)
> to whip or lash for the infliction of torture

Perhaps Pilate thought that scourging Jesus would move the hearts of the Jews so they would want to see Him released. But their hearts were hard (12:40), and they were determined to destroy Him. The crowd wanted him to die. They even asked that a common criminal, Barabbas, be released instead.

John 19:1–4

1   Then Pilate therefore took Jesus, and scourged him.
2   And the soldiers platted a crown of thorns, and put it on his head, and they put on him a purple robe,
3   And said, Hail, King of the Jews! And they smote him with their hands.
4   Pilate therefore went forth again, and saith unto them, Behold, I bring him forth to you, that ye may know that I find no fault in him.

John 18:38

38   Pilate saith unto him, What is truth? And when he had said this, he went out again unto the Jews, and saith unto them, I find in him no fault at all.

III. A Powerful Journey

Four times, Pilate had declared Jesus' innocence. Yet under public pressure, he gave in to the crowd and ordered Jesus to be crucified.

John 19:17–21

17   And he bearing his cross went forth into a place called the place of a skull, which is called in the Hebrew Golgotha:
18   Where they crucified him, and two other with him, on either side one, and Jesus in the midst.
19   And Pilate wrote a title, and put it on the cross. And the writing was, JESUS OF NAZARETH THE KING OF THE JEWS.
20   This title then read many of the Jews: for the place where Jesus was crucified was nigh to the city: and it was written in Hebrew, and Greek, and Latin.
21   Then said the chief priests of the Jews to Pilate, Write not, The King of the Jews; but that he said, I am King of the Jews.

Lesson Twelve—The Journey to the Cross

A. The power of love

Jesus bore His own cross on His journey to Golgatha, and He did so because of His great love for us. (Simon of Cyrene later came and carried it for Him.)

JOHN 19:17

17 *And he bearing his cross went forth into a place called the place of a skull, which is called in the Hebrew Golgotha:*

Jesus' life was not *taken* from Him by the cruel Roman guards or the religious leaders of the day. He willingly *gave* His life because He loved us.

ROMANS 5:6–8

6 *For when we were yet without strength, in due time Christ died for the ungodly.*
7 *For scarcely for a righteous man will one die: yet peradventure for a good man some would even dare to die.*
8 *But God commendeth his love toward us, in that, while we were yet sinners, Christ died for us.*

JOHN 15:13

13 *Greater love hath no man than this, that a man lay down his life for his friends.*

EPHESIANS 5:2

2 *And walk in love, as Christ also hath loved us, and hath given himself for us an offering and a sacrifice to God for a sweetsmelling savour.*

B. The power of humility

JOHN 19:18

18 *Where they crucified him, and two other with him, on either side one, and Jesus in the midst.*

The crucifixion of Christ bears record of the power of His humility. His humility was displayed as He was crucified between two thieves. The Bible says he was numbered with the transgressors.

ISAIAH 53:12
12 Therefore will I divide him a portion with the great, and he shall divide the spoil with the strong; because he hath poured out his soul unto death: and he was numbered with the transgressors; and he bare the sin of many, and made intercession for the transgressors.

Even though he was treated unfairly, Jesus still offered pardon from sins. We can thank the Lord that the first words from the Cross were words of forgiveness!

LUKE 23:34
34 Then said Jesus, Father, forgive them; for they know not what they do. And they parted his raiment, and cast lots.

Illustration

The story is told of an old preacher who had a dream about the crucifixion scene. In his dream, he was so disgusted with the treatment of His Saviour, that he went up to a Roman soldier and grabbed him from behind. When the soldier turned around, the preacher saw *his* face on the soldier! He then realized that his own sins had nailed Jesus to the Cross.

C. *The power of redemption*

JOHN 19:30
30 When Jesus therefore had received the vinegar, he said, It is finished: and he bowed his head, and gave up the ghost.

Lesson Twelve—The Journey to the Cross

The death of Jesus on the Cross meant that the payment for our sins had been made. The wages of our sin is death, and Jesus paid our sin when He died on the Cross.

Illustration

D.M. Stearns was preaching in Philadelphia. At the close of the service a stranger came up to him and said, "I don't like the way you spoke about the cross. I think that instead of emphasizing the death of Christ, it would be far better to preach Jesus, the teacher and example." Stearns replied, "If I presented Christ in that way, would you be willing to follow Him?" "I certainly would," said the stranger without hesitation. "All right then," said the preacher, "let's take the first step. He did no sin. Can you claim that for yourself?" The man looked confused and somewhat surprised. "Why, no," he said. "I acknowledge that I do sin." Stearns replied, "Then your greatest need is to have a Saviour, not an example!"

> **Redemption** (noun)
> The setting free of one who was in bondage, by paying his ransom price

Not only was the payment made, but atonement was accomplished! The famous Baptist pastor, R.G. Lee, visited Golgatha on a trip to the Holy Land. Dr. Lee wanted to go to the top of the hill but was discouraged by his guide. Eventually, Dr. Lee was permitted to walk up the hill. Finally, as they reached the top, the guide asked him, "Have you ever been here before?" Dr. Lee said, "Yes, some 2000 years ago."

Conclusion

MATTHEW 12:40

40 For as Jonas was three days and three nights in the whale's belly; so shall the Son of man be three days and three nights in the heart of the earth.

The crucifixion could have taken place on either a Thursday or Friday. Most people believe it to be Friday. During the three days Jesus was in the tomb, it may have seemed like Judas had won. It may have seemed like Pilate's indifference was the politically correct way to go.... But Sunday was coming!

> It's Friday
> Jesus is praying
> Peter is sleeping
> Judas is betraying
> But Sunday is coming

> It's Friday
> Pilate is struggling
> The council is conspiring
> The crowd is vilifying
> They don't even know that Sunday's coming

> It's Friday
> The disciples are running like sheep without a shepherd
> Mary is crying
> Peter is denying
> But they don't know that Sunday is a coming

> It's Friday
> The Romans beat my Jesus
> They robe Him in scarlet
> They crown Him with thorns
> But they don't know that Sunday's coming

Lesson Twelve—The Journey to the Cross

It's Friday
See Jesus walking to Calvary
His blood dripping
His body stumbling
And His spirit is burdened
But you see it's only Friday, Sunday's coming

It's Friday
The world's winning
People are sinning
And evil is grinning

It's Friday
The soldiers nailed my Saviour's hands to the cross
They nailed my Saviour's feet to the cross
And then they raised Him up next to criminals.

It's Friday
But let me tell you something
Sunday's coming

It's Friday
The disciples are questioning
What has happened to their King?
The Pharisees are celebrating that their
	scheming has been achieved.
But they don't know it's only Friday, Sunday's coming

It's Friday
He is hanging on the cross feeling forsaken by His Father
Left alone and dying
Can nobody save Him?
Oh, it's Friday, but Sunday's coming

It's Friday,
The earth trembles
The sky grows dark
My King yields His spirit

It's Friday
Hope is lost
Death has won
Sin has conquered
And Satan's just a laughing

It's Friday
Jesus is buried
A soldier stands guard
And a rock is rolled into place
But it's Friday
It is only Friday

Sunday is a coming.
—S.M. LOCKRIDGE

Your journey of faith is a lifelong journey. God knows exactly where you are on your personal journey. His main purpose is to make you more like Christ. Your purpose must be to glorify God by fulfilling His mission for your life. There will be trials. We will experience pain, but *Heaven* is coming! If Jesus endured the journey of the Cross, may we be willing to endure this journey today. May we look for the hope of Heaven and may we claim the power of the Gospel message!

ROMANS 1:16

16 For I am not ashamed of the gospel of Christ: for it is the power of God unto salvation to every one that believeth; to the Jew first, and also to the Greek.

LESSON TWELVE—THE JOURNEY TO THE CROSS

Study Questions

1. What is the definition of omniscient?
   God is omniscient which means He is all-knowing.

   1 JOHN 3:20
   For if our heart condemn us, God is greater than our heart, and knoweth all things.

2. How was the journey to the Cross personal for Jesus?
   It was planned by God the Father before the world began.

3. What was the first and main purpose of Jesus' death on the Cross?
   Jesus died on the Cross for the purpose of offering salvation to those who would believe.

4. In addition to offering salvation, what other purpose did Jesus' death on the Cross serve?
   Jesus glorified His Father by dying on the Cross.

5. Write out 1 Corinthians 6:20, and list two specific ways in which you can glorify God this week.

   1 CORINTHIANS 6:20
   For ye are bought with a price: therefore glorify God in your body, and in your spirit, which are God's.

   Answers will vary.

6. From whom did Jesus experience personal betrayal?
   Jesus was betrayed by Judas and denied by Peter, both followers of Him.

7. List three practical ways in which you can "stand with Jesus" in a world that denies Him.
   Answers will vary.

8. How did Jesus display humility from the Cross?
   He was hung between two thieves, and He offered forgiveness to those who crucified Him.

Memory Verse

2 CORINTHIANS 5:15

15 And that he died for all, that they which live should not henceforth live unto themselves, but unto him which died for them, and rose again.

LESSON THIRTEEN

The Journey to the Tomb

Key Verses
Luke 24:1–8

Lesson Overview
Jesus died on the Cross and, for His followers, all hope died with Him. He was placed in a tomb, and the tomb was sealed. The crucifixion was the ultimate of shattered dreams. There would be no kingdom. There would be no king. After days of mourning, Mary Magdalene, Mary the mother of Jesus, and other ladies were making a journey to the tomb to pay their last respects to the One in whom they had placed all of their hope. When they arrived, the stone was rolled away and two angels appeared to them proclaiming the news that Jesus had risen. Bewildered, they ran to tell Jesus' disciples the wonderful news.

Lesson Aim
By examining the events surrounding the burial and resurrection of Christ, we should seek to understand that as we claim the promises of God and practice the presence of Christ, He can turn sorrow into joy on our journeys of faith, and transform us in the process!

Lesson Goals

At the conclusion of this lesson, students should:
- Strive to remember and trust the promises of God.
- Turn to God and His Word when dealing with fear and sorrow.
- Understand the complete forgiveness offered by the Lord when we sin.
- Acknowledge the transformation that takes place at salvation.

Teaching Outline

I. A Sorrowful Journey
    A. Sorrowing the Saviour's death
    B. Surprised by the empty tomb

II. A Wonderful Journey
    A. Their fears were relieved.
        1. By the Word of God
        2. By the presence of Christ
    B. Their sorrow was removed.

III. A Transformational Journey
    A. Transformed through forgiveness
        1. Peter denied the Lord.
        2. Peter was forgiven by the Lord.
    B. Transformed through faith
        1. We are saved through faith.
        2. We are redeemed by faith.

LESSON THIRTEEN

The Journey to the Tomb

Text
Luke 24:1–8

Introduction
Placed amidst rambling townhouses in flat, sunny Houston, Texas, is a large building. It is the size of an airplane hangar. The purpose of this unconventional museum is to honor "one of our most important cultural rituals." It is the National Museum of Funeral History. There are no creaking doors or cobwebs in the corner. What one finds is a display of funeral memorabilia. Among the unusual items on display are a solid glass coffin, a casket for three, and a collection of hand-painted coffins from Ghana, Africa. Small signs throughout the museum warn, "Do not open caskets."

The large display of funeral vehicles includes a sleek black funeral sleigh, hearses that carried famous people, and even a 1916 Packard funeral bus. The funeral bus, designed to eliminate the funeral procession, carried the coffin, pallbearers, and twenty mourners. The bus was used only once. While climbing the hills of San Francisco during a funeral, the weight of all the people and the coffin caused the bus to overturn, spilling the people and the coffin onto the street.

While this is a bizarre museum, and we may wonder whether the parking lot is ever filled with visitors, the truth is that the burial of a person is the last way we can honor the one who died. After Jesus' death and burial, several women came to honor Him with spices and oils. Praise the Lord, the difference between Jesus and others who die, is that Jesus did not stay in the grave.

John 19:16–19
16 *Then delivered he him therefore unto them to be crucified. And they took Jesus, and led him away.*
17 *And he bearing his cross went forth into a place called the place of a skull, which is called in the Hebrew Golgotha:*
18 *Where they crucified him, and two other with him, on either side one, and Jesus in the midst.*
19 *And Pilate wrote a title, and put it on the cross. And the writing was, JESUS OF NAZARETH THE KING OF THE JEWS.*

One can only imagine the devastation felt by the early disciples of Jesus Christ as they stood at the foot of the Cross. At the end of the crucifixion, they made their journey to His tomb. These steps are the earliest of the Christian faith, though some, no doubt, thought they were the last.

Lesson Thirteen—The Journey to the Tomb

> **TEACHING TIP**
>
> *Order of the Events:*
> Mary Magdalene and other followers of Jesus journey to the tomb (Luke 23:55–24:1). Mary arrives before the other women in the party, sees the tomb opened, assumes that someone took His body, and runs off (John 20:1–2). The other women find the stone rolled away and the tomb empty (Luke 24:2–9). Mary Magdalene leaves to tell the disciples (John 20:1–2). Mary, the mother of James, draws closer and sees the angel. She goes back to meet the other women following with spices (Matthew 28:1–2). Peter and John arrive at the tomb, see that it is empty, and leave for their homes (John 20:3–10). Mary Magdalene returns, weeping. She sees the two angels and then Jesus (John 20:11–18). The risen Christ tells her to tell the disciples (John 20:17–18). Mary (mother of James) meanwhile returns with the women (Luke 24:1–4). They return and see the two angels (Luke 24:5; Mark 16:5). They also hear the angel's message (Matthew 28:6–8). On their way to find the disciples, they are met by the risen Christ (Matthew 28:9–10). Later in the afternoon, two disciples walk with Jesus and break bread with Him (Luke 24:13–31). Jesus appears in the evening in the upper room to the eleven (Luke 24:36–48; John 20:19–31).

I. A Sorrowful Journey

The disciples and followers of Jesus were devastated. As they stood at the foot of the Cross, their anticipation of a coming kingdom vanished. Jesus had been crucified. They had left everything to follow Him. They had walked with Him daily for three years. Their hearts must have been filled with confusion, fear, and apprehension. Their dreams seemed to be shattered. Their hope seemed to be gone. They seemed to have nothing left.

We begin with Mary Magdalene and others journeying to the tomb. It was a sad, fearful time for Mary (Jesus' mother), Mary Magdalene, and the other ladies as they walked toward the place of His burial.

> **TEACHING TIP**
>
> *It is interesting to note that these ladies were the last ones at the Cross and first to go to the tomb.*

MARK 16:10
10 And she went and told them that had been with him, as they mourned and wept.

A. *Sorrowing the Saviour's death*

LUKE 24:1
1 Now upon the first day of the week, very early in the morning, they came unto the sepulchre, bringing the spices which they had prepared, and certain others with them.

When Jesus met Mary Magdalene (Luke 8), she was plagued by demons. He set her free and gave her new life.

LUKE 8:2
2 And certain women, which had been healed of evil spirits and infirmities, Mary called Magdalene, out of whom went seven devils,

Mary Magdalene was changed from one who was separated from God by sin to one who found hope through forgiveness. Mark 16:9 says, "*Now when Jesus*

Lesson Thirteen—The Journey to the Tomb

was risen early the first day of the week, he appeared first to Mary Magdalene, out of whom he had cast seven devils." By God's mercy and through Jesus' death, burial, and resurrection, Mary Magdalene had a growing relationship with God through Jesus Christ. Now she faced the fear of life without the Lord Jesus. She sorrowed the death of the one who had changed her life forever.

B. Surprised by the empty tomb

LUKE 24:2–5
2 And they found the stone rolled away from the sepulchre.
3 And they entered in, and found not the body of the Lord Jesus.
4 And it came to pass, as they were much perplexed thereabout, behold, two men stood by them in shining garments:
5 And as they were afraid, and bowed down their faces to the earth,

JOHN 20:1–4
1 The first day of the week cometh Mary Magdalene early, when it was yet dark, unto the sepulchre, and seeth the stone taken away from the sepulchre.
2 Then she runneth, and cometh to Simon Peter, and to the other disciple, whom Jesus loved, and saith unto them, They have taken away the Lord out of the sepulchre, and we know not where they have laid him.
3 Peter therefore went forth, and that other disciple, and came to the sepulchre.
4 So they ran both together: and the other disciple did outrun Peter, and came first to the sepulchre.

Jesus had most certainly foretold of His own death, burial and resurrection, but sometimes in a trial we can lose perspective on the facts, and fear can hinder our ability to remember the promises of God.

JOHN 2:19

19 Jesus answered and said unto them, Destroy this temple, and in three days I will raise it up.

MATTHEW 26:31–32

31 Then saith Jesus unto them, All ye shall be offended because of me this night: for it is written, I will smite the shepherd, and the sheep of the flock shall be scattered abroad.
32 But after I am risen again, I will go before you into Galilee.

His followers were planning to place spices on Jesus' body in one last demonstration of their honor and love for the One who was dead. Their hearts were broken. When they arrived, they found the stone had been rolled away. As they looked inside, they found the tomb empty. Dismayed and surprised by the disappearance of Jesus, their despair increased. They had forgotten God's promise to them!

Illustration

A story is told of a group of primary aged children who had a "Show and Tell" demonstration at their school.

The first boy was called to the front of the class and said, "My name is Benjamin. I am Jewish, and this is the Star of David."

Next, a little girl was summoned to the front of the room, and she said, "My name is Mary. I am Roman Catholic, and this is a crucifix."

Lesson Thirteen—The Journey to the Tomb

Finally a little boy came to the front and said, "My name is Johnny. I am a Baptist, and this is a casserole."

Johnny was a little off when it came to identifying a great symbol of Baptists! He hadn't gotten it yet. He missed the truth of the Baptist's belief. In much the same way, the disciples hadn't gotten it yet when they came looking for Jesus. They did not realize the empty tomb was a great symbol testifying to the promises of God!

May we not be like Johnny or the followers of Christ who missed the point spiritually. May we not be surprised when God fulfills His Word!

II. A Wonderful Journey

LUKE 24:8
8 *And they remembered his words,*

Finally, Mary and those who were with her remembered His words! The journey is always wonderful when we remember His Words! When we gather together around God's Word in a Sunday school class, in a church service, or as a family, we find perspective and great joy!

A. Their fears were relieved

Their fears were relieved by the Word of God. Psalm 119:24 says, *"Thy testimonies also are my delight and my counsellors."*

Illustration

A very nervous airline passenger began pacing the terminal when bad weather delayed his flight. During his walk, he ran across one of those life insurance machines. It offered $100,000 in the event of an untimely death aboard his flight. The policy was just three dollars.

He looked out the window at the threatening clouds and thought of his family at home. For that price it was foolish not to buy, so he bought the coverage. He then looked for a place to eat and settled on his favorite, Chinese. It was a relaxing meal until he opened his fortune cookie. It read, "Your recent investment will pay big dividends."

In an effort to relieve his fears in his own strength, this man multiplied them! May we remember the words found in the New Testament, *"For God hath not given us the spirit of fear; but of power, and of love, and of a sound mind"* (2 Timothy 1:7).

They were not only relieved by the Word of Jesus, but also by the presence of Christ!

Luke 24:36–39

36 And as they thus spake, Jesus himself stood in the midst of them, and saith unto them, Peace be unto you.

37 But they were terrified and affrighted, and supposed that they had seen a spirit.

38 And he said unto them, Why are ye troubled? and why do thoughts arise in your hearts?

39 Behold my hands and my feet, that it is I myself: handle me, and see; for a spirit hath not flesh and bones, as ye see me have.

If we can learn anything from the Resurrection, it is that Jesus will always be with us! And when Jesus is with us, we experience great peace. The pyramids in Egypt are famous because they contain the mummified bodies of ancient Egyptian kings. Westminster Abbey in London is well known because of English nobles and notables who

Lesson Thirteen—The Journey to the Tomb

are laid to rest there. Arlington cemetery in Washington D.C. is revered as the honored resting place of many great Americans. We can thank the Lord that the tomb of Jesus is famous because it is empty!

Because the tomb is empty, our hearts can be filled with the presence of Christ! Jesus promises that He will never leave us or forsake us. Truly, it is a wonderful journey when we recognize that we are not alone!

B. Their sorrow was removed

LUKE 24:8–9

8 And they remembered his words,

9 And returned from the sepulchre, and told all these things unto the eleven, and to all the rest.

When Jesus arose, He planted the only durable rumor of hope amidst the widespread despair of a hopeless world.

Have your dreams been shattered? Are you confused or fearful? Are circumstances overwhelming you? When we try to figure it out on our own, nothing makes sense. When your life seems to be falling apart, you can transform your sorrowful journey into a joyful journey by turning to God's Word for help and strength. Whatever your burden is, the answer is found in the Bible.

What will you turn to to relieve your sorrow and hopelessness? The world turns to drugs, alcohol, and immorality. May we as Christians turn to our Saviour, for only then, will we find true relief from our sorrow and despair.

III. A Transformational Journey

A. *Transformed through forgiveness*

We learned last week that Peter had walked away from the Lord. He had denied Christ three times.

MARK 14:66–72

66 And as Peter was beneath in the palace, there cometh one of the maids of the high priest:

67 And when she saw Peter warming himself, she looked upon him, and said, And thou also wast with Jesus of Nazareth.

68 But he denied, saying, I know not, neither understand I what thou sayest. And he went out into the porch; and the cock crew.

69 And a maid saw him again, and began to say to them that stood by, This is one of them.

70 And he denied it again. And a little after, they that stood by said again to Peter, Surely thou art one of them: for thou art a Galilaean, and thy speech agreeth thereto.

71 But he began to curse and to swear, saying, I know not this man of whom ye speak.

72 And the second time the cock crew. And Peter called to mind the word that Jesus said unto him, Before the cock crow twice, thou shalt deny me thrice. And when he thought thereon, he wept.

Disheartened by his disloyalty, Peter undoubtedly wondered whether Jesus would ever forgive and use him again. Peter walked away from the crucifixion most likely in despair, knowing that he had failed. Nevertheless, the Lord forgave Peter. The angel gave a message to the disciples telling them where to wait to see Jesus. He included a special message to Peter that He would see him in Galilee.

Lesson Thirteen—The Journey to the Tomb

Mark 16:6–7

6 And he saith unto them, Be not affrighted: Ye seek Jesus of Nazareth, which was crucified: he is risen; he is not here: behold the place where they laid him.
7 But go your way, tell his disciples and Peter that he goeth before you into Galilee: there shall ye see him, as he said unto you.

God forgave Peter, and Peter was transformed as a result of that forgiveness.

If you are a Christian who has failed God, the Devil will say, "You blew it. Give up! You will never be able to serve God again." However, God was not finished with Peter, and He is not finished with you! He can forgive you and transform your life. God's forgiveness is complete.

1 John 1:9

9 If we confess our sins, he is faithful and just to forgive us our sins, and to cleanse us from all unrighteousness.

God not only forgives but also chooses not to remember our sin. It is remembered no more. Psalm 103:12 says, "*As far as the east is from the west, so far hath he removed our transgressions from us.*" God did not just forgive Peter but also restored him back into fellowship. He wanted to see and talk with Peter again.

When God forgives, He receives us back into fellowship. Psalm 103:2–4 says, "*Bless the Lord, O my soul, and forget not all his benefits: Who forgiveth all thine iniquities; who healeth all thy diseases; Who redeemeth thy life from destruction; who crowneth thee with lovingkindness and tender mercies.*" God longs to restore us into complete fellowship with Him.

B. Transformed through faith

John 20:24–29

24 But Thomas, one of the twelve, called Didymus, was not with them when Jesus came.
25 The other disciples therefore said unto him, We have seen the Lord. But he said unto them, Except I shall see in his hands the print of the nails, and put my finger into the print of the nails, and thrust my hand into his side, I will not believe.
26 And after eight days again his disciples were within, and Thomas with them: then came Jesus, the doors being shut, and stood in the midst, and said, Peace be unto you.
27 Then saith he to Thomas, Reach hither thy finger, and behold my hands; and reach hither thy hand, and thrust it into my side: and be not faithless, but believing.
28 And Thomas answered and said unto him, My Lord and my God.
29 Jesus saith unto him, Thomas, because thou hast seen me, thou hast believed: **blessed are they that have not seen, and yet have believed.**

We can thank the Lord that the ultimate life transformation takes place when we are saved through faith! In order to be transformed through faith in salvation, we must believe the truth about ourselves: we are sinners in need of forgiveness.

Romans 3:23–24

23 For all have sinned, and come short of the glory of God;
24 Being justified freely by his grace through the redemption that is in Christ Jesus:

Illustration

A Jew and a Christian were indulging in a friendly argument about their respective faiths. "Most of the good things you Christians have, you've taken from us," the Jew said. "The Ten Commandments, for instance." "I'll admit we took the Ten Commandments from you," answered the Christian, "but you can't say that we've kept them." (from *Nelson's Big Book of Laughter* by Lowell D. Streiker)

No person can keep all Ten Commandments, because we are sinners. The Ten Commandments weren't meant to simply be kept. They were meant to show us our need for a Saviour.

Not only must we believe the truth about ourselves, we must believe the truth about Jesus Christ!

John 11:25

25 Jesus said unto her, I am the resurrection, and the life: he that believeth in me, though he were dead, yet shall he live:

Jesus redeems us when we come to Him by faith. Redemption speaks not only of our forgiveness of sin, but our eternity with the Lord.

1 Corinthians 15:19–20

19 If in this life only we have hope in Christ, we are of all men most miserable.
20 But now is Christ risen from the dead, and become the firstfruits of them that slept.

Conclusion

JOHN 14:1–6

1 Let not your heart be troubled: ye believe in God, believe also in me.

2 In my Father's house are many mansions: if it were not so, I would have told you. I go to prepare a place for you.

3 And if I go and prepare a place for you, I will come again, and receive you unto myself; that where I am, there ye may be also.

4 And whither I go ye know, and the way ye know.

5 Thomas saith unto him, Lord, we know not whither thou goest; and how can we know the way?

6 Jesus saith unto him, I am the way, the truth, and the life: no man cometh unto the Father, but by me.

Our core beliefs about Jesus Christ and His death, burial, and resurrection must be the foundation of our faith. As we journey through our Christian life, we will face disappointment and shattered dreams. However, our faith will draw us closer to God. When tempted to doubt or wander from the path that glorifies God, we must remember the countless promises God has given us in His Word and claim those promises as we continue on our journeys for the faith.

Lesson Thirteen—The Journey to the Tomb

Study Questions

1. What is the one obvious difference between the death of Jesus and the death of other religious leaders and humans throughout the world?
   The obvious difference between the death of Jesus and the death of others throughout time is that Jesus rose from the grave.

2. Explain how God had worked in Mary Magdelene's life prior to her journey to the tomb.
   Jesus cast out seven devils from her body, healing her of evil spirits and infirmities.

3. Name two ways our fears can be relieved.
   Our fears are relieved when we remember the Word of God and acknowledge the presence of Christ in our daily lives.

4. Give one reference that proves Jesus had promised He would rise again.
   JOHN 2:19
   19 Jesus answered and said unto them, Destroy this temple, and in three days I will raise it up.

   MATTHEW 26:31–32
   31 Then saith Jesus unto them, All ye shall be offended because of me this night: for it is written, I will smite the shepherd, and the sheep of the flock shall be scattered abroad.
   32 But after I am risen again, I will go before you into Galilee.

5. List three ways you can remember the words and promises of God.
   Answers will vary, but may include the following:
   Listening to Bible teaching and preaching, spending personal time in Bible reading and prayer on a daily basis, displaying Scripture verses for quick reference throughout the day (3x5 cards, etc.)

6. When God forgives, He receives us back into fellowship with Himself. Look up Psalm 103:2–4 and list the four actions performed by God, proving His complete forgiveness.
   Psalm 103:2–4
   2 Bless the Lord, O my soul, and forget not all his benefits:
   3 Who forgiveth all thine iniquities; who healeth all thy diseases;
   4 Who redeemeth thy life from destruction; who crowneth thee with lovingkindness and tender mercies;

   He forgives, He heals, He redeems, He crowns us with lovingkindess and tender mercies.

7. What is the ultimate transformation that can take place in our lives because of the death and resurrection of Jesus?
   The ultimate transformation that takes place in our lives is salvation through faith.

   John 11:25
   25 Jesus said unto her, I am the resurrection, and the life: he that believeth in me, though he were dead, yet shall he live:

Lesson Thirteen—The Journey to the Tomb

8. Take a moment to think of the fears or sorrows you are facing in your life right now. List two promises (including Scripture references) you can claim from God's Word to help you experience the joy Jesus offers. *Answers will vary.*

Memory Verse

John 11:25

25 Jesus said unto her, I am the resurrection, and the life: he that believeth in me, though he were dead, yet shall he live:

For additional Christian
growth resources visit
www.strivingtogether.com